55 Japanese Appetizer Recipes for Home

By: Kelly Johnson

Table of Contents

- Edamame with Sea Salt
- Miso Soup with Tofu and Wakame
- Gyoza (Japanese Dumplings)
- Ebi Tempura (Shrimp Tempura)
- Agedashi Tofu (Deep-Fried Tofu)
- Yakitori (Grilled Chicken Skewers)
- Chawanmushi (steamed Egg Custard)
- Tsukemono (Pickled Vegetables)
- Tuna Tataki
- Sunomono (Cucumber Salad)
- Tango Sushi (Sweet Omelette Sushi)
- Shishito Peppers with Ponzu Sauce
- Negimaki (Scallion Rolls)
- Hiyayakko (Chilled Tofu)
- Ikura (Salmon Roe) on Sushi Rice
- Nasu Dengaku (Miso-Glazed Eggplant)
- Ika Geso Karaage (Fried Squid Tentacles)
- Chawanushi (Savory Egg Custard)
- Agedashi Shrimp (Deep-Fried Shrimp)
- Yaki Imo (grilled Sweet Potatoes)
- Saba Narezushi (Mackerel Sushi)
- Okonomiyaki (Japanese Savory Pancake)
- Kani Salad (Crab Salad)
- Ankimo (Monkfish Liver)
- Hamachi Kama (Yellowtail Collar)
- Yuba Rolls (Tofu Skin Rolls)
- Kinpira Gobo (Braised Burdock Root)
- Maguro Tartare (tuna Tartare)
- Ebi Sunomono (Shrimp Vinegared Salad)
- Uni Shooter (Sea Urchin Shot)
- Zaru Soba (Cold Buckwheat Noodles)
- Horenso Gomaae (Spinach with Sesame Dressing)
- Shrimp Shumai (steamed Shrimp Dumplings)
- Kakiage (Vegetable Tempura Fritters)
- Hijiki Salad (Seaweed Salad)
- Tori Momo (Chicken Thigh Skewers)

- Yaki Nasu (Grilled Eggplant)
- Ise Ebi no Sashimi (Spiny Lobster Sashimi)
- Tako Sunomono (Octopus Vinegared Salad)
- Inari Sushi (Sweet Soy-Marinated Tofu Pockets)
- Sake Harasu (Salmon Belly Sashimi)
- Nikujaga Spring Rolls (Meat and Potato Spring Rolls)
- Miso Nasu (Miso-Glazed Eggplant)
- Kushiage (Deep-Fried Skewers)
- Wakame Salad (Seaweed Salad)
- Uni Gunkan (Sea Urchin Battleship Sushi)
- Yaki Onigiri (Grilled Rice Balls)
- Kinoko Butter Yaki (Butter-Sautéed Mushrooms)
- Takoyaki (Octopus Balls)
- Yudofu (Hot Tofu)
- Saba Misoni (Miso-Braised Mackerel)
- Nasu Dengaku (Miso-Glazed Eggplant)
- Ginnan (Ginkgo Nuts)
- Tamagoyaki (Japanese Sweet Omelette)
- Hokkigai Sashimi (Surf Clam Sashimi)

Edamame with Sea Salt

Ingredients:

- 2 cups fresh or frozen edamame (young soybeans)
- 1 tablespoon sea salt (adjust to taste)
- Water for boiling

Instructions:

Boil Edamame:
- If using fresh edamame, shell them. If using frozen edamame, thaw them. In a pot of boiling water, cook the edamame for 3-5 minutes until they are tender but still have a slight crunch.

Drain and Cool:
- Drain the edamame and immediately transfer them to a bowl of ice water. This helps in stopping the cooking process and preserves their vibrant green color.

Season with Sea Salt:
- Once cooled, remove the edamame from the ice water and pat them dry. Sprinkle the edamame generously with sea salt. Toss them gently to ensure even coating.

Serve:
- Transfer the seasoned edamame to a serving dish. They can be served warm or at room temperature.

Enjoy:
- Edamame with sea salt makes for a delightful and nutritious snack. Simply squeeze the pods to release the beans into your mouth. Discard the empty pods.

Optional Variations:
- Experiment with different salts such as Himalayan salt or flavored salts for unique twists. Add a squeeze of fresh lemon juice or sprinkle with chili flakes for extra flavor.

Note:

Edamame with sea salt is not only a delicious appetizer but also a great source of protein, fiber, and essential nutrients. It's a popular and healthy choice for a quick and satisfying snack.

Miso Soup with Tofu and Wakame

Ingredients:

- 4 cups dashi (Japanese soup stock)
- 1/4 cup miso paste (white or red miso)
- 1/2 cup cubed tofu (silken or firm)
- 2 tablespoons dried wakame seaweed
- 2 green onions, finely sliced
- 1 tablespoon soy sauce (optional, for extra flavor)
- 1 teaspoon mirin (optional, for sweetness)

Instructions:

Prepare Dashi:
- In a pot, bring the dashi to a gentle simmer over medium heat. If you don't have pre-made dashi, you can make it using kombu (dried kelp) and katsuobushi (bonito flakes).

Rehydrate Wakame:
- Place the dried wakame in a bowl of water and let it rehydrate for about 5 minutes. Drain and set aside.

Add Tofu:
- Once the dashi is simmering, add the cubed tofu to the pot. Allow it to simmer for another 2-3 minutes until the tofu is heated through.

Dissolve Miso Paste:
- In a small bowl, dissolve the miso paste in a ladleful of hot dashi. Stir until smooth.

Add Miso to Soup:
- Lower the heat and add the dissolved miso paste to the pot. Be careful not to boil the miso as high heat can destroy its flavor. Gently stir to incorporate.

Add Wakame:
- Add the rehydrated wakame to the soup. If you prefer a smoother texture, you can chop the wakame before adding.

Season the Soup:
- If desired, add soy sauce and mirin to the soup for additional flavor. Adjust according to your taste preference.

Simmer (Optional):

- Allow the soup to simmer for an additional 2-3 minutes, ensuring all ingredients are well-heated.

Serve:
- Ladle the miso soup into bowls, and garnish with finely sliced green onions.

Enjoy:
- Miso Soup with Tofu and Wakame is best enjoyed hot as a comforting and nutritious appetizer.

Note:

Miso soup is a versatile dish, and you can customize it by adding other ingredients like mushrooms, spinach, or sliced radishes. Adjust the miso paste quantity to your taste, as the intensity can vary between different types of miso.

Gyoza (Japanese Dumplings)

Ingredients:

For the Filling:

- 1 cup ground pork
- 1 cup napa cabbage, finely chopped
- 2 green onions, finely chopped
- 2 cloves garlic, minced
- 1 tablespoon fresh ginger, grated
- 1 tablespoon soy sauce
- 1 teaspoon sesame oil
- 1/2 teaspoon sugar
- Salt and pepper to taste

For the Wrapper:

- Gyoza or dumpling wrappers (round, thin)

For Dipping Sauce:

- 3 tablespoons soy sauce
- 2 tablespoons rice vinegar
- 1 teaspoon sesame oil
- 1 teaspoon sugar
- 1 green onion, finely sliced (for garnish)

Instructions:

1. Prepare Filling:

    Squeeze Excess Water:
    - Sprinkle a pinch of salt over the finely chopped napa cabbage and let it sit for 5 minutes. Squeeze out the excess water.

    Mix Ingredients:

- In a bowl, combine ground pork, chopped napa cabbage, green onions, garlic, ginger, soy sauce, sesame oil, sugar, salt, and pepper. Mix well until all ingredients are incorporated.

2. Assemble Gyoza:

   Place Wrapper:
   - Place a gyoza wrapper in your palm or on a clean surface.

   Add Filling:
   - Spoon a small amount of filling into the center of the wrapper (about 1 teaspoon).

   Fold and Seal:
   - Moisten the edges of the wrapper with water and fold it in half, creating a half-moon shape. Pleat the edges, pressing to seal.

   Repeat:
   - Repeat the process until all wrappers are filled.

3. Cook Gyoza:

   Pan-Fry:
   - Heat a non-stick skillet over medium-high heat. Add a small amount of oil. Place the gyoza in the pan in a single layer, ensuring they're not touching. Cook until the bottoms are golden brown.

   Steam:
   - Pour about 1/4 cup of water into the pan and immediately cover with a lid. Steam for 5-7 minutes or until the wrappers are translucent and the filling is cooked.

   Crisp Bottoms (Optional):
   - Uncover and let the gyoza cook for an additional 2-3 minutes to crisp the bottoms.

4. Prepare Dipping Sauce:

   Mix Ingredients:
   - In a small bowl, mix soy sauce, rice vinegar, sesame oil, and sugar. Stir until the sugar dissolves.

   Garnish:
   - Garnish the sauce with finely sliced green onions.

5. Serve and Enjoy:

> Arrange Gyoza:
> - Arrange the gyoza on a serving plate.
>
> Serve with Dipping Sauce:
> - Serve the gyoza hot with the dipping sauce on the side.
>
> Enjoy:
> - Enjoy these delicious homemade gyoza as an appetizer or part of a Japanese meal!

Note:

Feel free to experiment with the filling by adding ingredients like chopped shrimp, mushrooms, or water chestnuts for added texture and flavor.

Ebi Tempura (Shrimp Tempura)

Ingredients:

For the Tempura Batter:

- 1 cup all-purpose flour
- 1 cup ice-cold water
- 1 egg, lightly beaten
- 1/2 teaspoon baking soda
- Ice cubes

For the Shrimp:

- 12 large shrimp, peeled and deveined, leaving tails intact
- Salt and pepper to taste
- Cornstarch for coating

For Frying:

- Vegetable oil for deep frying

For Dipping Sauce:

- 1/2 cup dashi (Japanese soup stock)
- 3 tablespoons soy sauce
- 2 tablespoons mirin
- Grated daikon radish (optional, for serving)

Instructions:

1. Prepare Shrimp:

    Season Shrimp:
    - Season the peeled and deveined shrimp with salt and pepper.

    Coat with Cornstarch:
    - Lightly coat each shrimp with cornstarch, shaking off excess.

2. Make Tempura Batter:

Chill Ingredients:
- Place a bowl in the freezer for a few minutes to chill. Ensure the water is very cold.

Prepare Batter:
- In the chilled bowl, mix flour, ice-cold water, beaten egg, and baking soda. Add ice cubes to keep the batter cold. Stir the batter briefly; it's okay if there are lumps.

3. Fry Shrimp:

Heat Oil:
- Heat vegetable oil in a deep fryer or a large, deep pot to 340-350°F (170-180°C).

Dip and Fry:
- Dip each shrimp into the tempura batter, coating it completely. Carefully place the battered shrimp into the hot oil. Fry in batches to avoid overcrowding.

Cook Until Golden:
- Fry the shrimp for 2-3 minutes or until the tempura batter is golden and crispy.

Drain Excess Oil:
- Remove the shrimp with a slotted spoon and place them on a paper towel-lined plate to drain excess oil.

4. Make Dipping Sauce:

Combine Ingredients:
- In a small saucepan, combine dashi, soy sauce, and mirin. Heat over low heat until warmed through.

Serve with Grated Daikon:
- Optionally, serve the dipping sauce with grated daikon radish for added flavor.

5. Serve and Enjoy:

Arrange Tempura:
- Arrange the Ebi Tempura on a serving plate.

Serve Immediately:
- Serve the shrimp tempura immediately while it's hot and crispy.

Dip and Enjoy:
- Dip the tempura into the sauce and enjoy this classic Japanese dish!

Note:

Serve Ebi Tempura with a side of rice or enjoy it as part of a larger tempura assortment. The key to successful tempura is to keep the batter cold, and the oil hot for a light and crispy texture.

Agedashi Tofu (Deep-Fried Tofu)

Ingredients:

For the Tofu:

- 1 block (about 14 ounces) firm tofu
- Cornstarch for coating
- Vegetable oil for deep frying

For the Dashi Sauce:

- 1 cup dashi (Japanese soup stock)
- 2 tablespoons soy sauce
- 2 tablespoons mirin
- 1 tablespoon sake
- 1 teaspoon sugar

For Garnish:

- Grated daikon radish
- Finely chopped green onions
- Bonito flakes (katsuobushi)

Instructions:

1. Prepare Tofu:

    Drain Tofu:
    - Remove the tofu from the packaging and drain excess water. Wrap the tofu block in paper towels and gently press to remove more moisture.

    Cut Tofu:
    - Cut the tofu block into 8 equal cubes.

    Coat with Cornstarch:
    - Lightly coat each tofu cube with cornstarch, shaking off excess.

2. Fry Tofu:

Heat Oil:
- Heat vegetable oil in a deep fryer or a large, deep pot to 350-360°F (180-182°C).

Deep Fry:
- Carefully place the tofu cubes into the hot oil. Fry until they are golden brown and crispy. This usually takes about 3-4 minutes.

Drain Excess Oil:
- Use a slotted spoon to remove the fried tofu cubes and place them on a paper towel-lined plate to drain excess oil.

3. Make Dashi Sauce:

Combine Ingredients:
- In a small saucepan, combine dashi, soy sauce, mirin, sake, and sugar. Heat over low heat until warmed through. Do not bring it to a boil.

4. Serve Agedashi Tofu:

Arrange Tofu:
- Arrange the deep-fried tofu cubes on serving plates.

Pour Dashi Sauce:
- Pour the warm dashi sauce over the tofu cubes.

Garnish:
- Garnish the Agedashi Tofu with grated daikon radish, finely chopped green onions, and a sprinkle of bonito flakes.

Serve Immediately:
- Serve the Agedashi Tofu immediately while it's hot, ensuring the crispy exterior is preserved.

Note:

Agedashi Tofu is a popular appetizer in Japanese cuisine, known for its crispy exterior and soft interior. The combination of the warm dashi sauce and garnishes enhances the overall flavor. Enjoy this dish as a delightful and savory starter!

Yakitori (Grilled Chicken Skewers)

Ingredients:

For the Yakitori Sauce:

- 1/2 cup soy sauce
- 1/4 cup sake
- 1/4 cup mirin
- 2 tablespoons sugar
- 1 clove garlic, minced
- 1 teaspoon grated ginger

For the Chicken Skewers:

- 1 1/2 lbs (700g) boneless, skinless chicken thighs, cut into bite-sized pieces
- 1 cup green onions, cut into 1-inch pieces
- Bamboo skewers, soaked in water

For Garnish (Optional):

- Shichimi togarashi (Japanese seven-spice blend)
- Sesame seeds

Instructions:

1. Prepare Yakitori Sauce:

    Combine Ingredients:
    - In a saucepan, combine soy sauce, sake, mirin, sugar, minced garlic, and grated ginger. Bring to a simmer over medium heat, stirring until the sugar dissolves. Simmer for about 5 minutes, allowing the flavors to meld. Remove from heat and let it cool.

    Divide Sauce:
    - Reserve a portion of the sauce for basting during grilling.

2. Assemble Chicken Skewers:

Preheat Grill:
- Preheat your grill to medium-high heat.

Thread Chicken and Green Onions:
- Thread the chicken pieces and green onions alternately onto the soaked bamboo skewers.

3. Grill Yakitori:

Oil Grill Grates:
- Brush the grill grates with oil to prevent sticking.

Grill Skewers:
- Place the skewers on the preheated grill and cook for about 5-7 minutes, turning occasionally.

Baste with Sauce:
- Baste the skewers with the reserved Yakitori sauce during the last few minutes of grilling, ensuring the chicken gets a glossy glaze.

Check Doneness:
- Ensure the chicken is thoroughly cooked, with no pink in the center.

4. Serve Yakitori:

Arrange Skewers:
- Arrange the grilled Yakitori skewers on a serving platter.

Garnish (Optional):
- Sprinkle with shichimi togarashi and sesame seeds for added flavor and presentation.

Serve Hot:
- Serve the Yakitori skewers hot, either as an appetizer or as part of a main course.

Note:

Yakitori is a popular Japanese street food, and grilling the skewers imparts a delicious smoky flavor. The combination of the savory Yakitori sauce and the tenderness of the grilled chicken makes this dish a favorite among food enthusiasts. Enjoy the authentic taste of Japanese grilled chicken skewers!

Chawanmushi (steamed Egg Custard)

Ingredients:

- 3 large eggs
- 2 1/2 cups dashi (Japanese soup stock)
- 1 tablespoon soy sauce
- 1 tablespoon mirin
- 1/2 teaspoon salt
- 1 teaspoon sugar
- 1/2 cup chicken, cooked and shredded
- 4 large shrimp, peeled and deveined
- 1/2 cup fresh shiitake mushrooms, sliced
- 1/2 cup ginkgo nuts, peeled (optional)
- 1 green onion, finely sliced (for garnish)

Instructions:

1. Prepare Ingredients:

   Cook Chicken:
   - Cook chicken until fully done, then shred it into small pieces.

   Prepare Shrimp:
   - Peel and devein the shrimp.

   Slice Mushrooms:
   - Slice the shiitake mushrooms.

   Peel Ginkgo Nuts (Optional):
   - If using ginkgo nuts, peel and blanch them in hot water for a few minutes. Remove the inner skin.

2. Make Chawanmushi Mixture:

   Beat Eggs:
   - In a bowl, lightly beat the eggs.

   Combine Dashi, Soy Sauce, Mirin, Salt, and Sugar:
   - In another bowl, combine dashi, soy sauce, mirin, salt, and sugar. Mix well.

   Mix Eggs and Dashi Mixture:

- Gradually add the dashi mixture to the beaten eggs, stirring constantly to avoid forming bubbles.

3. Assemble Chawanmushi:

    Divide Ingredients:
    - Divide the shredded chicken, shrimp, sliced mushrooms, and ginkgo nuts (if using) into serving cups or bowls.

    Pour Egg Mixture:
    - Pour the egg and dashi mixture over the ingredients in each cup, filling them to about 80% full.

    Cover Cups:
    - Cover each cup with a piece of aluminum foil.

4. Steam Chawanmushi:

    Prepare Steamer:
    - Place the cups in a steamer or a large pot with a steaming rack.

    Steam:
    - Steam the Chawanmushi for about 15-20 minutes or until the custard is set. To check doneness, insert a toothpick into the custard, and if it comes out clean, it's ready.

5. Serve Chawanmushi:

    Garnish:
    - Garnish each Chawanmushi cup with a few shrimp, a sprinkle of sliced green onions, and additional ginkgo nuts if desired.

    Serve Warm:
    - Serve the Chawanmushi warm, either as an appetizer or a light main dish.

Note:

Chawanmushi is a delicate and savory Japanese steamed egg custard that can be customized with various ingredients. The silky texture of the custard, combined with the flavors of dashi, soy sauce, and mirin, makes it a delightful and comforting dish. Enjoy the rich and subtle taste of Chawanmushi!

Tsukemono (Pickled Vegetables)

Ingredients:

- Assorted vegetables (cucumber, radish, carrot, Napa cabbage, etc.)
- 1 tablespoon salt (for brining)
- 1 cup rice vinegar
- 1/2 cup sugar
- 1 teaspoon salt
- 1 piece kombu (dried kelp), about 2 inches
- 1 red chili pepper (optional, for heat)

Instructions:

1. Prepare Vegetables:

    Wash and Slice:
    - Wash the vegetables thoroughly. Slice them into thin strips, rounds, or any desired shape.

    Brine Vegetables:
    - In a large bowl, sprinkle 1 tablespoon of salt over the sliced vegetables. Toss to coat evenly and let them sit for about 30 minutes. This process helps draw out excess moisture from the vegetables.

2. Make Pickling Solution:

    Combine Vinegar, Sugar, Salt, and Kombu:
    - In a saucepan, combine rice vinegar, sugar, salt, and kombu. Heat over medium heat, stirring until the sugar and salt dissolve. Bring the mixture to a simmer, then remove it from heat.

    Cool Pickling Solution:
    - Let the pickling solution cool to room temperature. Remove the kombu and discard it.

3. Pickle Vegetables:

    Squeeze Excess Moisture:
    - After 30 minutes of brining, squeeze out the excess moisture from the vegetables.

    Pack Vegetables in Jars:

- Pack the squeezed vegetables tightly into clean, sterilized jars.

Add Pickling Solution:
- Pour the cooled pickling solution over the vegetables, ensuring they are fully submerged. If using, add a red chili pepper for a bit of heat.

Close Jars:
- Seal the jars tightly and refrigerate them.

4. Let Tsukemono Marinate:

Marinate in Refrigerator:
- Allow the tsukemono to marinate in the refrigerator for at least 24 hours. The longer they marinate, the more flavor they will absorb.

Shake or Stir Occasionally:
- Shake or stir the jars occasionally to ensure the pickling solution is distributed evenly.

5. Serve Tsukemono:

Drain Excess Liquid:
- Before serving, drain off excess liquid from the pickled vegetables.

Serve as a Side:
- Serve tsukemono as a side dish, garnish, or accompaniment to rice and other main dishes.

Note:

Tsukemono refers to a variety of Japanese pickled vegetables, and the selection of vegetables and pickling methods can vary. Feel free to experiment with different vegetables and adjust the level of sweetness or saltiness to suit your taste preferences. Enjoy the refreshing and tangy flavors of homemade tsukemono!

Tuna Tataki

Ingredients:

For the Tuna:

- 1 lb (450g) sushi-grade tuna
- 1 tablespoon soy sauce
- 1 tablespoon mirin
- 1 tablespoon sake
- 1 tablespoon sesame oil
- 1 teaspoon grated ginger
- 1 teaspoon sugar
- 1 tablespoon vegetable oil (for searing)

For the Dipping Sauce:

- 2 tablespoons soy sauce
- 1 tablespoon mirin
- 1 tablespoon rice vinegar
- 1 teaspoon sesame oil
- 1 teaspoon sesame seeds (optional)
- 1 green onion, finely sliced (for garnish)

Instructions:

1. Prepare Tuna:

    Slice Tuna:
    - Slice the sushi-grade tuna into 1/2-inch thick pieces.

    Marinate Tuna:
    - In a bowl, mix soy sauce, mirin, sake, sesame oil, grated ginger, and sugar. Coat the tuna slices with the marinade and let them marinate for about 15-20 minutes.

2. Sear Tuna:

    Heat Vegetable Oil:
    - Heat vegetable oil in a skillet or pan over high heat.

    Sear Tuna:

- Sear the marinated tuna slices quickly on each side, just until the edges are lightly browned. The goal is to sear the outside while keeping the inside rare.

Chill Tuna:
- Once seared, transfer the tuna to a plate and let it cool. Place it in the refrigerator for about 15-20 minutes to chill.

3. Make Dipping Sauce:

Combine Ingredients:
- In a small bowl, mix soy sauce, mirin, rice vinegar, sesame oil, and sesame seeds (if using). Stir until well combined.

4. Serve Tuna Tataki:

Slice and Arrange:
- Slice the chilled tuna thinly and arrange the slices on a serving plate.

Drizzle with Dipping Sauce:
- Drizzle the tuna slices with the dipping sauce.

Garnish:
- Garnish with finely sliced green onions.

Serve Immediately:
- Serve the Tuna Tataki immediately as an appetizer or part of a sushi platter.

Note:

Tuna Tataki is a Japanese dish where the outer layer of the tuna is seared, leaving the inside rare. The marinade adds a depth of flavor, and the dipping sauce complements the dish perfectly. Enjoy the delicate balance of textures and tastes in this elegant and flavorful appetizer!

Sunomono (Cucumber Salad)

Ingredients:

For the Cucumber Salad:

- 2 large cucumbers, thinly sliced
- 1 teaspoon salt
- 1/2 cup wakame seaweed, rehydrated (optional)
- 1/4 cup sliced red radishes (optional)
- Sesame seeds for garnish (optional)

For the Vinegar Dressing:

- 1/4 cup rice vinegar
- 2 tablespoons soy sauce
- 2 tablespoons sugar
- 1 teaspoon sesame oil
- 1 teaspoon grated ginger
- 1 teaspoon toasted sesame seeds

Instructions:

1. Prepare Cucumber Salad:

    Thinly Slice Cucumbers:
    - Slice the cucumbers thinly. You can use a mandoline for uniform slices.

    Salt Cucumbers:
    - Place the sliced cucumbers in a colander, sprinkle them with salt, and toss to coat evenly. Let them sit for about 15-20 minutes to release excess water.

    Rehydrate Wakame (Optional):
    - If using wakame seaweed, rehydrate it according to package instructions.

    Slice Radishes (Optional):
    - Slice the red radishes thinly.

2. Make Vinegar Dressing:

Combine Ingredients:
- In a bowl, mix rice vinegar, soy sauce, sugar, sesame oil, grated ginger, and toasted sesame seeds. Stir until the sugar dissolves.

3. Assemble Sunomono:

Squeeze Excess Water:
- After the cucumbers have released excess water, gently squeeze them to remove any remaining liquid.

Combine Ingredients:
- In a large bowl, combine the sliced cucumbers, rehydrated wakame, and sliced radishes.

Pour Dressing:
- Pour the vinegar dressing over the cucumber mixture. Toss gently to coat the vegetables evenly.

4. Chill and Serve:

Chill:
- Place the Sunomono in the refrigerator and let it chill for at least 30 minutes to allow the flavors to meld.

Garnish (Optional):
- Before serving, garnish the Sunomono with sesame seeds for added texture.

Serve Cold:
- Serve the Sunomono cold as a refreshing side dish or appetizer.

Note:

Sunomono is a light and refreshing Japanese cucumber salad that pairs well with various dishes. The combination of crisp cucumbers, umami from the seaweed, and the tangy-sweet vinegar dressing creates a delightful balance of flavors. Enjoy this cooling salad on warm days or as a palate cleanser during a meal.

Tango Sushi (Sweet Omelette Sushi)

Ingredients:

For the Sweet Omelette:

- 4 large eggs
- 2 tablespoons sugar
- 1 tablespoon mirin
- 1 tablespoon soy sauce
- Vegetable oil for cooking

For the Sushi Rice:

- 2 cups sushi rice, cooked and seasoned with rice vinegar, sugar, and salt

For Assembly:

- Nori (seaweed) sheets, cut into thin strips
- Pickled ginger (optional, for serving)
- Soy sauce (for dipping)

Instructions:

1. Prepare Sweet Omelette:

    Whisk Eggs:
    - In a bowl, whisk the eggs until well-beaten.

    Add Sugar, Mirin, and Soy Sauce:
    - Add sugar, mirin, and soy sauce to the beaten eggs. Whisk until the sugar dissolves.

    Cook Omelette:
    - Heat a non-stick skillet over medium heat and lightly oil it. Pour a thin layer of the egg mixture into the pan. Swirl the pan to spread the mixture evenly.

    Roll Omelette:
    - Once the edges are set, roll the omelette from one side to the other. Push the rolled omelette to the side of the pan.

    Oil Pan Again:
    - Oil the empty side of the pan and pour another thin layer of the egg mixture. Lift the rolled omelette to let the new mixture flow underneath.

Continue Rolling:
- Continue rolling the omelette until all the egg mixture is used. Once cooked, let it cool and slice into thin strips.

2. Assemble Tango Sushi:

Prepare Sushi Rice:
- Cook sushi rice and season it with rice vinegar, sugar, and salt. Let it cool to room temperature.

Place Nori Strips on Bamboo Mat:
- Lay out a bamboo sushi rolling mat and place thin strips of nori on it.

Spread Sushi Rice:
- Wet your hands and spread a thin layer of sushi rice over the nori strips.

Add Sweet Omelette Strips:
- Place strips of sweet omelette along the center of the rice.

Roll Sushi:
- Carefully roll the sushi using the bamboo mat as a guide. Seal the edge with a bit of water.

Slice into Bite-sized Pieces:
- Using a sharp knife, slice the roll into bite-sized pieces.

Repeat:
- Repeat the process with the remaining rice, nori, and sweet omelette.

3. Serve Tango Sushi:

Arrange on a Plate:
- Arrange the Tango Sushi on a serving plate.

Serve with Pickled Ginger and Soy Sauce:
- Serve with pickled ginger on the side and soy sauce for dipping.

Enjoy:
- Enjoy the unique and delightful flavors of Tango Sushi, where the sweet omelette adds a touch of sweetness to traditional sushi!

Note:

Tango Sushi is a playful and sweet twist on traditional sushi. The combination of the slightly sweet omelette and seasoned sushi rice creates a delightful harmony of flavors. It's a fun and creative option for those who enjoy experimenting with different sushi variations.

Shishito Peppers with Ponzu Sauce

Ingredients:

For Shishito Peppers:

- 1 pound shishito peppers
- 1 tablespoon vegetable oil
- Flaky sea salt for sprinkling

For Ponzu Sauce:

- 1/4 cup soy sauce
- 2 tablespoons fresh lemon juice
- 2 tablespoons fresh orange juice
- 1 tablespoon rice vinegar
- 1 tablespoon mirin
- 1 teaspoon sugar
- 1 teaspoon grated daikon radish (optional)
- 1 teaspoon finely chopped green onion (optional)

Instructions:

1. Prepare Shishito Peppers:

    Wash and Dry:
    - Wash the shishito peppers and pat them dry with a paper towel.

    Heat Oil:
    - Heat vegetable oil in a large skillet or pan over medium-high heat.

    Sauté Peppers:
    - Add the shishito peppers to the hot skillet and sauté them, tossing occasionally, until they blister and char on the edges. This usually takes about 5-7 minutes.

    Sprinkle with Salt:
    - Once the shishito peppers are blistered, transfer them to a serving plate and sprinkle with flaky sea salt.

2. Make Ponzu Sauce:

    Combine Ingredients:

- In a bowl, whisk together soy sauce, fresh lemon juice, fresh orange juice, rice vinegar, mirin, and sugar until well combined.

Add Optional Ingredients:
- Optionally, add grated daikon radish and finely chopped green onion to the ponzu sauce. Stir to incorporate.

3. Serve Shishito Peppers with Ponzu Sauce:

Arrange Peppers:
- Arrange the sautéed shishito peppers on a serving plate.

Drizzle with Ponzu Sauce:
- Drizzle the ponzu sauce over the shishito peppers.

Serve Immediately:
- Serve the Shishito Peppers with Ponzu Sauce immediately as a flavorful appetizer or snack.

Note:

Shishito Peppers with Ponzu Sauce make for a delicious and simple appetizer with a perfect balance of flavors. The slightly sweet and tangy ponzu sauce complements the smoky and mildly spicy shishito peppers. This dish is popular in Japanese cuisine and is a great addition to any appetizer spread or as a side dish. Enjoy the delightful combination of flavors and textures!

Negimaki (Scallion Rolls)

Ingredients:

For the Beef Rolls:

- 1 pound thinly sliced beef (flank steak or sirloin)
- 1 bunch scallions (green onions), trimmed
- Salt and black pepper to taste

For the Marinade/Sauce:

- 1/2 cup soy sauce
- 1/4 cup mirin
- 2 tablespoons sake
- 2 tablespoons sugar
- 1 teaspoon grated ginger
- 1 teaspoon minced garlic
- Sesame seeds for garnish (optional)

Instructions:

1. Prepare Beef and Scallions:

    Slice Beef Thinly:
    - If the beef is not already thinly sliced, you can ask your butcher to slice it for you. Alternatively, place the beef in the freezer for about 30 minutes to make it easier to slice thinly.

    Trim Scallions:
    - Trim the ends of the scallions and cut them into lengths that match the width of the beef slices.

2. Assemble Negimaki:

    Season Beef:
    - Lay the beef slices flat and season them with a pinch of salt and black pepper.

    Place Scallions:
    - Place a few scallion pieces on each beef slice.

    Roll Up:

- Roll the beef slices around the scallions to create a tight roll. Secure the end with toothpicks.

3. Make Marinade/Sauce:

    Combine Ingredients:
    - In a bowl, mix together soy sauce, mirin, sake, sugar, grated ginger, and minced garlic. This will serve as both the marinade and the sauce.

4. Marinate and Cook Negimaki:

    Marinate Rolls:
    - Place the beef rolls in a shallow dish and pour half of the marinade over them. Let them marinate for at least 30 minutes.

    Cook on Grill or Pan:
    - Grill the beef rolls on an outdoor grill or in a grill pan over medium-high heat until the beef is cooked and the scallions are tender. Baste with the remaining marinade/sauce during cooking.

    Alternatively, Broil:
    - Preheat your oven's broiler. Place the beef rolls on a broiler pan and broil for a few minutes on each side until the beef is cooked and has a nice char.

5. Garnish and Serve:

    Garnish with Sesame Seeds:
    - Garnish the Negimaki with sesame seeds if desired.

    Remove Toothpicks:
    - Before serving, remove the toothpicks from the rolls.

    Serve Hot:
    - Serve the Negimaki hot as an appetizer or part of a Japanese-inspired meal.

Note:

Negimaki is a classic Japanese dish featuring thinly sliced beef rolled around scallions and grilled or broiled to perfection. The marinade/sauce adds a savory-sweet flavor to the dish. It's a popular choice in Japanese restaurants and is a delightful appetizer or side dish. Enjoy the savory and tender goodness of Negimaki!

Hiyayakko (Chilled Tofu)

Ingredients:

- 1 block (about 14 ounces) silken or soft tofu
- Soy sauce for drizzling
- 1 tablespoon finely chopped green onions (scallions)
- 1 tablespoon grated ginger
- Bonito flakes (katsuobushi) for garnish (optional)
- Toasted sesame seeds for garnish (optional)

Instructions:

1. Prepare Tofu:

    Cut Tofu:
    - Carefully remove the tofu from its packaging and cut it into serving-sized blocks. Use a sharp knife to cut the tofu gently to avoid breaking it.

    Drain Excess Water:
    - If there is excess water, drain it by placing the tofu blocks on a plate lined with paper towels for a few minutes.

2. Serve Hiyayakko:

    Plate Tofu:
    - Place the tofu blocks on individual serving plates.

    Drizzle Soy Sauce:
    - Drizzle a generous amount of soy sauce over each tofu block.

    Sprinkle Green Onions and Ginger:
    - Sprinkle finely chopped green onions and grated ginger over the tofu.

3. Garnish (Optional):

    Add Bonito Flakes:
    - If desired, top the tofu with bonito flakes for added umami. The heat of the tofu will cause the bonito flakes to gently dance on top.

    Sprinkle Sesame Seeds:

- Optionally, sprinkle toasted sesame seeds over the tofu for a nutty flavor.

4. Serve Chilled:

   Chill:
   - Place the assembled Hiyayakko in the refrigerator for a short time if you prefer it extra chilled.

   Serve Immediately:
   - Serve the Hiyayakko immediately as a refreshing and simple appetizer or side dish.

Note:

Hiyayakko is a popular Japanese dish known for its simplicity and refreshing taste. The chilled tofu is a perfect canvas for the savory soy sauce, aromatic green onions, and zesty ginger. Customize the toppings based on your preferences, and enjoy this light and cool dish, especially during hot weather or as a quick and healthy appetizer.

Ikura (Salmon Roe) on Sushi Rice

Ingredients:

- Sushi rice, prepared (vinegared rice seasoned with sugar and salt)
- Ikura (salmon roe)
- Soy sauce (for drizzling, optional)
- Nori strips (optional)
- Wasabi (optional)
- Pickled ginger (optional)

Instructions:

1. Prepare Sushi Rice:

    Cook Sushi Rice:
    - Prepare sushi rice according to the package instructions or your preferred method. Season the rice with a mixture of rice vinegar, sugar, and salt while it's still warm.

    Cool and Fluff Rice:
    - Allow the sushi rice to cool to room temperature. Once cooled, fluff the rice gently with a rice paddle or wooden spoon to separate the grains.

2. Serve Ikura on Sushi Rice:

    Place Sushi Rice:
    - Scoop a small portion of sushi rice onto individual serving plates or bowls.

    Top with Ikura:
    - Generously top the sushi rice with a layer of ikura (salmon roe).

    Optional Garnishes:
    - If desired, you can add optional garnishes like a drizzle of soy sauce, nori strips, a small amount of wasabi, or pickled ginger.

3. Serve and Enjoy:

    Serve Immediately:

- Serve the Ikura on Sushi Rice immediately to enjoy the vibrant flavors and textures.

Savor the Delicacy:
- Experience the burst of briny flavor from the ikura as it combines with the seasoned sushi rice. The optional garnishes can add extra layers of taste to enhance the dish.

Note:

Ikura on Sushi Rice is a classic Japanese dish that showcases the rich and flavorful salmon roe over a bed of seasoned sushi rice. The combination of the delicate, popping texture of the ikura and the seasoned rice creates a delightful harmony of flavors. Enjoy this elegant and indulgent dish as a special treat or part of a sushi feast!

Nasu Dengaku (Miso-Glazed Eggplant)

Ingredients:

- 2 large Japanese eggplants (or 4 small ones)
- 2 tablespoons white miso paste
- 1 tablespoon mirin
- 1 tablespoon sake
- 1 tablespoon sugar
- 1 tablespoon vegetable oil
- Sesame seeds for garnish
- Chopped green onions for garnish (optional)

Instructions:

1. Prepare Eggplants:

    Cut Eggplants:
    - Cut the eggplants in half lengthwise. Make shallow diagonal cuts on the surface of each half to create a crosshatch pattern.

    Preheat Oven:
    - Preheat your oven's broiler.

2. Make Miso Glaze:

    Mix Miso Glaze:
    - In a bowl, mix together white miso paste, mirin, sake, and sugar until well combined.

3. Glaze and Broil Eggplants:

    Brush with Oil:
    - Brush the cut sides of the eggplants with vegetable oil.

    Broil Eggplants:
    - Place the eggplants on a baking sheet, cut side up, and broil them for about 5 minutes or until they begin to soften and the edges char slightly.

    Apply Miso Glaze:
    - Remove the eggplants from the oven and spread the miso glaze evenly over the cut sides.

    Broil Again:

- Return the eggplants to the broiler and cook for an additional 3-5 minutes, or until the miso glaze is caramelized and bubbly.

4. Garnish and Serve:

    Garnish:
    - Sprinkle sesame seeds over the miso-glazed eggplants. Optionally, garnish with chopped green onions for added freshness.

    Serve Hot:
    - Serve the Nasu Dengaku hot as a flavorful appetizer or side dish.

Note:

Nasu Dengaku, or Miso-Glazed Eggplant, is a popular Japanese dish known for its sweet and savory miso glaze. The broiling process creates a tender and creamy texture in the eggplant while caramelizing the miso glaze to perfection. Enjoy this dish as a delightful appetizer or side, showcasing the rich flavors of miso and the natural sweetness of eggplant.

Ika Geso Karaage (Fried Squid Tentacles)

Ingredients:

- 1 pound squid tentacles (ika geso), cleaned and pat dry
- 1 cup potato starch or cornstarch
- Vegetable oil for frying
- Salt and pepper to taste
- Lemon wedges for serving
- Shichimi togarashi (Japanese seven-spice blend) for additional seasoning (optional)

Instructions:

1. Prepare Squid Tentacles:

    Clean Squid Tentacles:
    - Ensure that the squid tentacles are cleaned thoroughly. Pat them dry with paper towels.

    Season with Salt and Pepper:
    - Season the squid tentacles with salt and pepper to taste.

2. Coat with Potato Starch:

    Dredge in Potato Starch:
    - In a bowl, coat each squid tentacle with potato starch or cornstarch, shaking off any excess.

3. Fry Squid Tentacles:

    Heat Oil:
    - In a deep fryer or a large, deep pot, heat vegetable oil to 350°F (175°C).

    Fry in Batches:
    - Carefully lower the coated squid tentacles into the hot oil, frying them in batches for about 2-3 minutes or until they turn golden brown and crispy.

    Drain Excess Oil:
    - Use a slotted spoon to remove the fried squid tentacles from the oil and place them on a plate lined with paper towels to drain excess oil.

4. Serve Ika Geso Karaage:

Season and Serve Hot:
- While still hot, season the fried squid tentacles with a sprinkle of salt and pepper. Optionally, you can use shichimi togarashi for an extra kick.

Serve with Lemon Wedges:
- Serve the Ika Geso Karaage hot with lemon wedges on the side for a citrusy touch.

Enjoy as an Appetizer:
- Enjoy the crispy and flavorful Ika Geso Karaage as a delightful appetizer or snack.

Note:

Ika Geso Karaage is a delicious Japanese dish featuring fried squid tentacles that are crispy on the outside and tender on the inside. The light coating of potato starch or cornstarch adds to the crunchiness, making it a popular izakaya (Japanese pub) dish. Serve these flavorful bites with a squeeze of lemon for a delightful burst of citrus.

Chawanushi (Savory Egg Custard)

Ingredients:

Note: The ingredient quantities can be adjusted based on the number of servings.

- 2 cups dashi (Japanese soup stock)
- 4 large eggs
- 1 tablespoon soy sauce
- 1 tablespoon mirin
- 1/2 teaspoon salt
- 1/2 teaspoon sugar
- 1/2 cup cooked chicken, shredded
- 1/2 cup shrimp, peeled and deveined
- 1/2 cup shiitake mushrooms, sliced
- 1/2 cup ginkgo nuts (optional)
- 4 small gingko leaves or mitsuba (Japanese wild parsley) for garnish
- Soy sauce for drizzling (optional)

Instructions:

1. Prepare Ingredients:

    Prepare Dashi:
    - Make dashi by combining dashi granules or bonito flakes with water. Strain to remove any solid particles.

    Prepare Ingredients:
    - Cook and prepare the chicken, shrimp, shiitake mushrooms, and ginkgo nuts if using.

2. Make Chawanmushi Mixture:

    Beat Eggs:
    - In a bowl, beat the eggs gently. Be careful not to create too many bubbles.

    Combine Seasonings:
    - Add soy sauce, mirin, salt, and sugar to the beaten eggs. Mix well.

    Gradually Add Dashi:
    - Gradually add the dashi to the egg mixture while stirring continuously to avoid creating bubbles.

    Strain Mixture:

- Strain the egg mixture through a fine-mesh sieve into another bowl. This helps achieve a smooth and silky texture.

3. Assemble and Steam:

    Divide Ingredients:
    - Divide the cooked chicken, shrimp, shiitake mushrooms, and ginkgo nuts among individual chawanmushi cups or small heatproof bowls.

    Pour Egg Mixture:
    - Pour the strained egg mixture over the ingredients in each cup.

    Cover and Steam:
    - Cover each cup with a lid or aluminum foil. Steam the chawanmushi cups in a steamer for about 15-20 minutes or until the custard is set. You can check for doneness by inserting a toothpick; if it comes out clean, the chawanmushi is ready.

4. Garnish and Serve:

    Garnish:
    - Garnish each chawanmushi with a small gingko leaf or mitsuba.

    Serve Warm:
    - Serve the chawanmushi warm. Optionally, drizzle a bit of soy sauce on top before serving.

    Enjoy:
    - Enjoy the delicate and savory Chawanmushi as a comforting appetizer or light meal.

Note:

Chawanmushi is a traditional Japanese dish known for its silky-smooth texture and rich umami flavor. It's a versatile dish that can include a variety of ingredients. The key to a perfect chawanmushi is achieving a delicate custard texture through careful steaming. Feel free to customize the ingredients based on your preferences and enjoy this comforting dish served in small cups or bowls.

Agedashi Shrimp (Deep-Fried Shrimp)

Ingredients:

For the Shrimp:

- 1 pound large shrimp, peeled and deveined
- Salt and pepper to taste
- 1 cup all-purpose flour, for dredging
- 2 large eggs, beaten
- 2 cups Panko breadcrumbs

For the Dashi Broth:

- 2 cups dashi (Japanese soup stock)
- 2 tablespoons soy sauce
- 2 tablespoons mirin
- 1 tablespoon sake
- 1 teaspoon sugar

For Garnish:

- Finely chopped green onions
- Grated daikon radish
- Shichimi togarashi (Japanese seven-spice blend)
- Chopped fresh cilantro (optional)
- Tempura dipping sauce (optional)

Instructions:

1. Prepare Shrimp:

   Season Shrimp:
   - Season the peeled and deveined shrimp with salt and pepper.

   Dredge in Flour:
   - Dredge each shrimp in all-purpose flour, shaking off any excess.

   Coat in Egg:
   - Dip the floured shrimp in beaten eggs.

   Cover in Panko:

- Coat the shrimp with Panko breadcrumbs, pressing the breadcrumbs onto the shrimp to adhere.

2. Fry Shrimp:

    Heat Oil:
    - Heat vegetable oil in a deep fryer or a large, deep pot to 350°F (175°C).

    Fry in Batches:
    - Carefully lower the coated shrimp into the hot oil, frying them in batches for about 2-3 minutes or until they turn golden brown and crispy.

    Drain Excess Oil:
    - Use a slotted spoon to remove the fried shrimp from the oil and place them on a plate lined with paper towels to drain excess oil.

3. Make Dashi Broth:

    Combine Ingredients:
    - In a saucepan, combine dashi, soy sauce, mirin, sake, and sugar. Heat over low heat until warmed through. Do not bring it to a boil.

4. Serve Agedashi Shrimp:

    Arrange Shrimp:
    - Arrange the fried shrimp in serving bowls.

    Pour Dashi Broth:
    - Pour the warm dashi broth over the fried shrimp, allowing the broth to soak into the Panko coating.

    Garnish:
    - Garnish the Agedashi Shrimp with finely chopped green onions, grated daikon radish, shichimi togarashi, and optional cilantro.

    Serve Immediately:
    - Serve the Agedashi Shrimp immediately, with optional tempura dipping sauce on the side.

Note:

Agedashi Shrimp is a delightful Japanese dish where crispy and golden-fried shrimp are served in a warm and savory dashi broth. The contrast of the crispy exterior with the tender shrimp and the umami-rich broth makes it a popular choice. Garnish with fresh ingredients for added flavor and enjoy this dish as an appetizer or part of a Japanese-inspired meal.

Yaki Imo (grilled Sweet Potatoes)

Ingredients:

- Sweet potatoes (Japanese sweet potatoes are traditionally used)
- Optional: Butter or honey for serving

Instructions:

1. Choose Sweet Potatoes:

    Select Sweet Potatoes:
    - Choose sweet potatoes suitable for grilling. Japanese sweet potatoes, with their purple skin and creamy interior, are commonly used for Yaki Imo.

2. Prepare Sweet Potatoes:

    Wash and Scrub:
    - Wash the sweet potatoes thoroughly and scrub off any dirt. You can leave the skin on for added flavor.

    Soak in Water (Optional):
    - Some people soak the sweet potatoes in water for a couple of hours before grilling. This step is optional and can help enhance the sweetness and moisture.

3. Grill Sweet Potatoes:

    Preheat Grill:
    - Preheat your grill to medium heat.

    Wrap in Foil (Optional):
    - Optionally, you can wrap each sweet potato in aluminum foil. This method helps to steam the potatoes, making them tender on the inside.

    Place on Grill:
    - Place the sweet potatoes directly on the grill grates or in the foil if using. Close the grill lid.

    Grill Until Tender:
    - Grill the sweet potatoes for about 30-40 minutes, turning them occasionally to ensure even cooking. They are ready when a fork easily pierces through the flesh.

4. Serve Yaki Imo:

   Cool Slightly:
   - Allow the grilled sweet potatoes to cool slightly before serving.

   Peel and Enjoy:
   - Peel the skin off the sweet potatoes if desired. The skin is edible and adds extra flavor.

   Serve Warm:
   - Serve the Yaki Imo warm. Optionally, you can drizzle them with melted butter or honey for added richness and sweetness.

Note:

Yaki Imo, or grilled sweet potatoes, is a popular autumn and winter treat in Japan. The grilling process enhances the natural sweetness of the potatoes, creating a delicious and comforting snack. Enjoy the warm and tender Yaki Imo on a chilly day for a delightful and satisfying experience.

Saba Narezushi (Mackerel Sushi)

Ingredients:

For the Narezushi:

- 2 cups sushi rice, prepared
- 2 fillets mackerel (saba), deboned and salted
- 1 cup nuka-zuke (rice bran pickles)
- Bamboo leaves (optional, for wrapping)

For the Nuka-zuke (Rice Bran Pickles):

- 2 cups rice bran
- 1 cup salt
- 1 cup sake lees (sake kasu)
- 2 tablespoons soy sauce
- 1 tablespoon mirin
- Mackerel bones and scraps (optional, for added flavor)

Instructions:

1. Prepare Nuka-zuke (Rice Bran Pickles):

    Combine Ingredients:
    - In a large bowl, combine rice bran, salt, sake lees, soy sauce, mirin, and optional mackerel bones and scraps. Mix well.

    Add Mackerel:
    - Rub the mackerel fillets with the nuka-zuke mixture, making sure they are well coated. Place them in a container, cover with the remaining nuka-zuke, and refrigerate for 2-3 days.

2. Assemble Saba Narezushi:

    Prepare Bamboo Leaves (Optional):
    - If using bamboo leaves, blanch them in hot water and cut into rectangular pieces.

Remove Mackerel from Nuka-zuke:
- Take the mackerel fillets out of the nuka-zuke, removing excess pickling mixture.

Slice Mackerel:
- Slice the mackerel fillets into thin pieces.

Assemble Sushi:
- On a plate or sushi mat, spread a layer of sushi rice. Place slices of pickled mackerel on top of the rice.

Wrap with Bamboo Leaves (Optional):
- Optionally, wrap the sushi with bamboo leaves, securing them with string or a strip of seaweed.

3. Serve Saba Narezushi:

Slice and Serve:
- Slice the Saba Narezushi into individual servings and serve on a plate.

Enjoy:
- Enjoy the unique flavors of this traditional style of fermented mackerel sushi.

Note:

Saba Narezushi is a traditional style of sushi where mackerel is fermented with rice bran pickles. The pickling process gives the mackerel a distinctive flavor and texture. This style of sushi is less common than the more widely known vinegared rice sushi. The use of nuka-zuke, or rice bran pickles, adds depth and complexity to the dish. Enjoy this unique and traditional Japanese culinary experience.

Okonomiyaki (Japanese Savory Pancake)

Ingredients:

For the Batter:

- 2 cups all-purpose flour
- 1 ½ cups dashi (Japanese soup stock)
- 2 large eggs
- 1 teaspoon soy sauce
- 1 teaspoon mirin
- 1/2 teaspoon salt
- 1/2 cabbage, finely shredded
- 4 green onions, finely chopped

For the Filling (Optional, Choose Your Favorites):

- 1 cup cooked and chopped pork belly or bacon
- 1/2 cup tenkasu (tempura scraps) or tempura flakes
- 1/2 cup small shrimp, peeled and deveined

For Toppings:

- Okonomiyaki sauce
- Japanese mayonnaise
- Aonori (seaweed flakes)
- Katsuobushi (bonito flakes)

Instructions:

1. Prepare the Batter:

   Combine Dry Ingredients:
   - In a large bowl, whisk together the all-purpose flour and salt.

   Add Wet Ingredients:
   - In a separate bowl, mix dashi, eggs, soy sauce, and mirin. Gradually add the wet ingredients to the dry ingredients, whisking to avoid lumps.

   Add Vegetables:
   - Add finely shredded cabbage and chopped green onions to the batter. Mix until well combined.

2. Cook Okonomiyaki:

   Preheat Griddle or Pan:
   - Preheat a griddle or a large non-stick pan over medium heat.

   Spoon Batter:
   - Spoon the batter onto the griddle, forming round pancake shapes (about 1/2 to 1 inch thick).

   Add Filling (Optional):
   - If desired, add your choice of filling ingredients such as chopped pork belly or bacon, tenkasu (tempura scraps), and small shrimp on top of the batter.

   Cook Both Sides:
   - Cook the okonomiyaki for about 5-7 minutes on each side, or until golden brown and cooked through.

3. Serve Okonomiyaki:

   Transfer to Plate:
   - Transfer the cooked okonomiyaki to a serving plate.

   Add Toppings:
   - Drizzle okonomiyaki sauce and Japanese mayonnaise over the top. Sprinkle aonori (seaweed flakes) and katsuobushi (bonito flakes) as desired.

   Slice and Enjoy:
   - Slice the okonomiyaki into wedges and enjoy it while hot.

Note:

Okonomiyaki is a versatile Japanese dish often referred to as a "Japanese savory pancake" or "Japanese pizza." It allows for a variety of fillings and toppings, making it customizable to personal preferences. The combination of the savory batter, crisp edges, and flavorful toppings creates a delightful and comforting dish. Experiment with different fillings and toppings to suit your taste.

Kani Salad (Crab Salad)

Ingredients:

- 1 cup imitation crab meat, shredded
- 1/2 cucumber, julienned
- 1/2 carrot, julienned
- 1/4 cup mayonnaise
- 1 teaspoon soy sauce
- 1 teaspoon rice vinegar
- 1/2 teaspoon sugar
- 1/2 teaspoon sesame oil
- Sesame seeds for garnish (optional)
- Chopped chives or green onions for garnish (optional)
- Avocado slices for serving (optional)

Instructions:

1. Prepare Vegetables:

   Julienne Cucumber and Carrot:
   - Using a julienne peeler or knife, cut the cucumber and carrot into thin, matchstick-like strips.

2. Make Kani Salad:

   Combine Crab Meat and Vegetables:
   - In a bowl, combine the shredded imitation crab meat, julienned cucumber, and julienned carrot.

   Prepare Dressing:
   - In a separate bowl, whisk together mayonnaise, soy sauce, rice vinegar, sugar, and sesame oil until well combined.

   Combine Salad and Dressing:
   - Pour the dressing over the crab and vegetable mixture. Gently toss until everything is evenly coated with the dressing.

3. Serve Kani Salad:

   Chill (Optional):

- You can refrigerate the Kani Salad for about 15-30 minutes to chill and enhance the flavors.

Garnish:
- Optionally, garnish the salad with sesame seeds, chopped chives or green onions.

Serve with Avocado (Optional):
- Serve the Kani Salad on a plate and optionally arrange slices of avocado around the salad.

Enjoy:
- Serve the Kani Salad as a refreshing and delicious appetizer or side dish.

Note:

Kani Salad is a popular Japanese dish that features imitation crab meat and crunchy vegetables in a creamy and flavorful dressing. It's a light and refreshing salad that is easy to prepare and perfect for warm weather. Feel free to customize the ingredients and adjust the dressing to suit your taste preferences.

Ankimo (Monkfish Liver)

Ingredients:

- 1 fresh monkfish liver (about 1 pound)
- 1/4 cup sake
- 1/4 cup mirin
- 1/4 cup soy sauce
- 1 teaspoon sugar
- Wasabi (for serving)
- Thinly sliced green onions (for garnish)

Instructions:

1. Prepare Monkfish Liver:

    Clean Monkfish Liver:
    - Rinse the monkfish liver under cold water and carefully remove any membranes or connective tissues.

    Poach Monkfish Liver:
    - In a pot, bring water to a gentle simmer. Place the monkfish liver in a heatproof dish or a foil-lined basket, and steam or poach it for about 20-30 minutes until it becomes firm and cooked through.

    Cool and Press:
    - Allow the cooked monkfish liver to cool to room temperature. Optionally, you can press it under a weight to shape it into a firm block.

2. Prepare Ankimo Sauce:

    Combine Sake, Mirin, Soy Sauce, and Sugar:
    - In a small saucepan, combine sake, mirin, soy sauce, and sugar. Heat over low heat, stirring until the sugar dissolves. Allow the mixture to cool.

3. Serve Ankimo:

    Slice Monkfish Liver:
    - Slice the cooled monkfish liver into thin rounds.

    Drizzle with Sauce:
    - Arrange the ankimo slices on a plate and drizzle the sauce over them.

    Garnish:

- Garnish with thinly sliced green onions.

Serve with Wasabi:
- Serve ankimo with a side of wasabi.

Note:

Ankimo is a traditional Japanese dish made from the liver of monkfish. Often referred to as "foie gras of the sea," ankimo has a delicate and rich flavor. It is typically served chilled with a savory sauce. Enjoy this delicacy as an appetizer or part of a traditional Japanese kaiseki meal.

Hamachi Kama (Yellowtail Collar)

Ingredients:

- 1 yellowtail collar (hamachi kama)
- Salt for seasoning
- Soy sauce for serving
- Lemon wedges for serving
- Optional: Grated daikon radish for serving

Instructions:

1. Prepare Yellowtail Collar:

    Thaw (if frozen):
    - Ensure the yellowtail collar is properly thawed if it was frozen.

    Pat Dry:
    - Pat the yellowtail collar dry with paper towels.

2. Season and Grill:

    Preheat Grill:
    - Preheat a grill to medium-high heat.

    Season with Salt:
    - Season both sides of the yellowtail collar generously with salt.

    Grill Yellowtail Collar:
    - Place the yellowtail collar on the preheated grill. Grill each side for about 10-15 minutes, or until the skin is crispy and the flesh is cooked through. You can use a grill pan or an outdoor grill.

    Check for Doneness:
    - To check if it's done, insert a fork or skewer into the thickest part of the collar. The flesh should easily flake off, and the internal temperature should be around 145°F (63°C).

3. Serve Hamachi Kama:

    Plate and Serve:
    - Transfer the grilled yellowtail collar to a serving platter.

    Serve with Accompaniments:

- Serve the hamachi kama with soy sauce on the side for dipping. Squeeze fresh lemon juice over the collar before eating. Optionally, you can serve it with grated daikon radish for added freshness.

Enjoy:
- Enjoy the delicious and flavorful hamachi kama, savoring the tender and succulent meat near the collar bone.

Note:

Hamachi Kama, or yellowtail collar, is a prized and flavorful part of the fish. Grilling it brings out the natural richness and tenderness of the meat, while the crispy skin adds an extra layer of texture. It's a popular dish in Japanese cuisine and is often enjoyed as a delicacy.

Yuba Rolls (Tofu Skin Rolls)

Ingredients:

For the Yuba Rolls:

- Yuba (tofu skin sheets)
- Vegetables (e.g., carrots, cucumbers, avocado, sprouts)
- Cooked sushi rice
- Nori sheets (optional)

For the Dipping Sauce:

- Soy sauce
- Rice vinegar
- Mirin
- Wasabi (optional)
- Grated ginger (optional)

Instructions:

1. Prepare Ingredients:

    Cut Vegetables:
    - Julienne or thinly slice your choice of vegetables. Common choices include carrots, cucumbers, avocado, and sprouts.

    Cook Sushi Rice:
    - Cook sushi rice according to the package instructions and let it cool to room temperature.

    Prepare Yuba Sheets:
    - If using dried yuba sheets, rehydrate them according to the package instructions. If using fresh yuba sheets, ensure they are soft and pliable.

2. Assemble Yuba Rolls:

    Lay Out Yuba Sheets:
    - Lay out a yuba sheet on a clean surface.

Layer with Nori (Optional):
- Optionally, place a small piece of nori on the yuba sheet if you want to include seaweed in your rolls.

Spread Sushi Rice:
- Spread a thin layer of sushi rice evenly over the yuba sheet, leaving a small border at the top.

Arrange Vegetables:
- Arrange julienned vegetables along the bottom edge of the yuba sheet.

Roll Up:
- Roll the yuba sheet from the bottom, enclosing the vegetables and rice. Roll it tightly but gently to avoid tearing the yuba.

Seal Edge:
- Seal the edge with a bit of water to secure the roll.

Repeat:
- Repeat the process for the remaining yuba sheets and filling ingredients.

3. Slice and Serve:

Slice Yuba Rolls:
- Use a sharp knife to slice the yuba rolls into bite-sized pieces.

Arrange on Plate:
- Arrange the sliced yuba rolls on a serving plate.

4. Prepare Dipping Sauce:

Mix Ingredients:
- In a small bowl, mix soy sauce, rice vinegar, mirin, and, if desired, a bit of grated ginger and wasabi to taste.

5. Serve Yuba Rolls:

Serve with Dipping Sauce:
- Serve the yuba rolls with the dipping sauce on the side.

Enjoy:
- Enjoy these refreshing and nutritious yuba rolls as a light and tasty appetizer or snack.

Note:

Yuba rolls are a delicious and vegan-friendly alternative to traditional sushi rolls. The yuba (tofu skin) adds a unique texture, and you can customize the filling to suit your taste. These rolls are not only flavorful but also a great source of plant-based protein. Serve them with a tasty dipping sauce for a delightful and healthy treat.

Kinpira Gobo (Braised Burdock Root)

Ingredients:

- 1 to 2 burdock roots (gobo)
- 1 carrot
- 1 tablespoon sesame oil
- 2 tablespoons soy sauce
- 1 tablespoon mirin
- 1 tablespoon sake
- 1 tablespoon sugar
- 1 tablespoon sesame seeds (optional, for garnish)

Instructions:

1. Prepare Ingredients:

    Peel and Julienne Burdock Root:
    - Peel the burdock root and cut it into thin, matchstick-sized pieces. Place the cut burdock root in a bowl of water with a splash of vinegar to prevent discoloration.

    Peel and Cut Carrot:
    - Peel the carrot and cut it into thin, matchstick-sized pieces.

2. Cook Kinpira Gobo:

    Heat Sesame Oil:
    - In a large skillet or wok, heat sesame oil over medium heat.

    Add Burdock Root:
    - Drain the burdock root and add it to the hot oil. Stir-fry for a few minutes until the burdock becomes glossy.

    Add Carrot:
    - Add the julienned carrot to the skillet and continue to stir-fry for another couple of minutes.

    Combine Soy Sauce, Mirin, Sake, and Sugar:
    - In a small bowl, mix together soy sauce, mirin, sake, and sugar.

    Pour Sauce Over Vegetables:
    - Pour the sauce mixture over the burdock root and carrot. Stir well to ensure even coating.

Simmer:
- Reduce the heat to low, cover the skillet, and let the vegetables simmer for about 15-20 minutes, or until they become tender. Stir occasionally.

3. Garnish and Serve Kinpira Gobo:

Check for Doneness:
- Taste the burdock root and carrot to ensure they are tender and have absorbed the flavors.

Adjust Seasoning:
- Adjust the seasoning if necessary by adding more soy sauce or sugar.

Garnish with Sesame Seeds:
- If desired, garnish with sesame seeds for added flavor and texture.

Serve:
- Serve kinpira gobo as a side dish or over a bowl of steamed rice. It can be enjoyed warm or at room temperature.

Note:

Kinpira Gobo is a classic Japanese dish that features burdock root and carrots braised in a sweet and savory soy-based sauce. The dish is known for its crunchy texture and rich flavor. It can be served as a side dish, enjoyed in bento boxes, or used as a topping for rice. Adjust the seasoning to your taste preferences, and feel free to experiment with additional ingredients like shiitake mushrooms or konnyaku for variation.

Maguro Tartare (Tuna Tartare)

Ingredients:

- 1/2 pound sushi-grade tuna, finely diced
- 1 tablespoon soy sauce
- 1 teaspoon sesame oil
- 1 teaspoon mirin
- 1 teaspoon rice vinegar
- 1 teaspoon ginger, finely grated
- 1 green onion, finely chopped
- 1/2 avocado, diced
- 1 teaspoon sesame seeds (optional, for garnish)
- Nori strips or wonton crisps (for serving)

Instructions:

1. Prepare Tuna:

    Dice Tuna:
    - Using a sharp knife, finely dice the sushi-grade tuna into small, uniform cubes.

    Marinate Tuna:
    - In a bowl, combine the diced tuna with soy sauce, sesame oil, mirin, rice vinegar, and grated ginger. Gently toss to ensure the tuna is well coated. Allow it to marinate for a few minutes.

2. Assemble Maguro Tartare:

    Add Green Onion and Avocado:
    - Add finely chopped green onion and diced avocado to the marinated tuna. Gently mix to combine.

    Adjust Seasoning:
    - Taste the tartare and adjust the seasoning if needed by adding more soy sauce, sesame oil, or other ingredients according to your preference.

3. Serve Maguro Tartare:

Plate the Tartare:
- Using a ring mold or by shaping it with a spoon, plate the maguro tartare on individual serving plates.

Garnish:
- If desired, sprinkle sesame seeds on top for garnish.

Serve with Nori or Wonton Crisps:
- Serve the maguro tartare with strips of nori or crispy wonton crisps on the side.

Enjoy:
- Enjoy the maguro tartare as a refreshing and elegant appetizer.

Note:

Maguro Tartare is a stylish and flavorful dish featuring fresh, raw tuna marinated in a savory and umami-rich sauce. It's often served as an appetizer or a light meal. The combination of sushi-grade tuna, avocado, and Asian-inspired seasonings creates a delicious and visually appealing dish. Serve it with nori strips or crispy wonton crisps for added texture and enjoy the delicate flavors of this tuna tartare.

Ebi Sunomono (Shrimp Vinegared Salad)

Ingredients:

For the Sunomono:

- 12 medium shrimp, peeled and deveined
- 1 cucumber, thinly sliced
- 1/4 cup wakame seaweed, rehydrated (optional)
- 2 tablespoons sesame seeds (optional, for garnish)

For the Vinegar Dressing:

- 1/4 cup rice vinegar
- 2 tablespoons soy sauce
- 2 tablespoons mirin
- 1 tablespoon sugar
- 1 teaspoon sesame oil

Instructions:

1. Prepare Shrimp:

    Boil Shrimp:
    - Bring a pot of water to a boil. Add the peeled and deveined shrimp, and cook for 1-2 minutes or until they turn pink and opaque. Remove from heat, drain, and let them cool.

    Slice Shrimp:
    - Once the shrimp are cooled, slice them in half horizontally.

2. Prepare Cucumber and Wakame:

    Slice Cucumber:
    - Thinly slice the cucumber. If using wakame seaweed, rehydrate it according to the package instructions.

3. Make Vinegar Dressing:

Mix Dressing Ingredients:
- In a small bowl, whisk together rice vinegar, soy sauce, mirin, sugar, and sesame oil until the sugar is dissolved.

4. Assemble Ebi Sunomono:

Combine Ingredients:
- In a mixing bowl, combine the sliced shrimp, cucumber slices, and rehydrated wakame seaweed (if using).

Pour Dressing:
- Pour the vinegar dressing over the shrimp and cucumber mixture. Toss gently to coat everything evenly with the dressing.

Chill (Optional):
- Refrigerate the sunomono for about 15-30 minutes to allow the flavors to meld and the salad to chill.

5. Garnish and Serve:

Plate the Sunomono:
- Plate the ebi sunomono on individual serving dishes or a larger serving platter.

Garnish with Sesame Seeds:
- If desired, garnish with sesame seeds for added texture.

6. Enjoy:

Serve Chilled:
- Serve the ebi sunomono chilled as a refreshing appetizer or side dish.

Enjoy the Freshness:
- Enjoy the crispness of cucumber, the sweetness of shrimp, and the tangy flavor of the vinegar dressing in this delightful sunomono salad.

Note:

Ebi Sunomono is a light and refreshing Japanese salad featuring shrimp and cucumber in a sweet and tangy vinegar dressing. It's a perfect appetizer or side dish, especially during warm weather. The addition of wakame seaweed enhances the texture and adds a hint of ocean flavor. This dish is not only delicious but also visually appealing, making it a popular choice in Japanese cuisine.

Uni Shooter (Sea Urchin Shot)

Ingredients:

- Fresh sea urchin (uni) roe
- Sake or rice wine
- Soy sauce
- Wasabi (optional)
- Seaweed strips (optional, for garnish)

Instructions:

1. Prepare Sea Urchin:

    Open Sea Urchin:
    - Carefully open the sea urchin to extract the fresh roe (uni). Use a spoon to gently scoop out the uni from the shell.

2. Assemble Uni Shooter:

    Prepare Shot Glasses:
    - Pour a small amount of sake or rice wine into each shot glass.

    Add Sea Urchin Roe:
    - Carefully place a spoonful of fresh sea urchin roe (uni) into each shot glass with sake.

    Drizzle with Soy Sauce:
    - Drizzle a small amount of soy sauce over the sea urchin roe in each shot glass.

    Add Wasabi (Optional):
    - If desired, add a small amount of wasabi to each shot glass for a spicy kick.

3. Garnish and Serve:

    Garnish with Seaweed (Optional):
    - Garnish the Uni Shooter with seaweed strips for an extra touch of flavor and presentation.

    Serve Immediately:
    - Serve the Uni Shooter immediately while the ingredients are fresh and flavors are vibrant.

4. Enjoy:

> Sip or Shoot:
> - Sip the Uni Shooter slowly to savor the rich and briny flavor of the sea urchin roe. Alternatively, you can shoot it for a more intense experience.
>
> Appreciate the Delicacy:
> - Enjoy the unique and delicate taste of sea urchin in this exquisite shot.

Note:

Uni Shooter is a luxurious and indulgent way to enjoy fresh sea urchin roe. The combination of sake, soy sauce, and the rich, creamy texture of uni creates a delightful and sophisticated shot. The addition of wasabi provides a hint of heat, and seaweed garnish complements the oceanic flavors. This dish is often served as an appetizer in upscale seafood restaurants, allowing diners to appreciate the delicate and unique taste of sea urchin.

Zaru Soba (Cold Buckwheat Noodles)

Ingredients:

For the Soba Noodles:

- 8 ounces (about 230g) soba noodles
- Water for boiling
- Ice water for cooling

For the Dipping Sauce (Tsuyu):

- 1 cup dashi (Japanese soup stock)
- 1/3 cup soy sauce
- 1/3 cup mirin
- 1 tablespoon sugar

Optional Toppings:

- Green onions, finely chopped
- Wasabi
- Nori (seaweed), shredded
- Grated daikon radish

Instructions:

1. Cook Soba Noodles:

    Boil Water:
    - Bring a large pot of water to a boil.

    Cook Soba Noodles:
    - Cook the soba noodles according to the package instructions (usually about 5-7 minutes). Stir occasionally to prevent sticking.

    Drain and Rinse:
    - Once the noodles are cooked, drain them and rinse under cold running water to remove excess starch and cool them down.

    Ice Water Bath:
    - Transfer the rinsed soba noodles to a bowl of ice water to ensure they are thoroughly chilled. Let them sit in the ice water for a few minutes.

2. Prepare Dipping Sauce (Tsuyu):

   Combine Ingredients:
   - In a bowl, combine dashi, soy sauce, mirin, and sugar. Stir well until the sugar dissolves.

   Chill Tsuyu:
   - Optionally, you can chill the dipping sauce in the refrigerator for a more refreshing experience.

3. Serve Zaru Soba:

   Arrange Noodles:
   - Drain the chilled soba noodles and arrange them on a bamboo or mesh sieve (zaru) or individual plates.

   Serve with Toppings:
   - Optionally, serve the zaru soba with chopped green onions, wasabi, shredded nori, and grated daikon radish on the side.

   Dip and Enjoy:
   - Dip the cold soba noodles into the chilled dipping sauce (tsuyu) and enjoy the refreshing and nutty flavor of zaru soba.

Note:

Zaru Soba is a popular Japanese dish, especially during the warmer months. The cold buckwheat noodles are served with a flavorful dipping sauce called tsuyu. The dish is often garnished with toppings like green onions, wasabi, shredded nori, and grated daikon radish. Zaru soba is a light and refreshing meal, perfect for hot days. The dipping sauce adds a savory and umami-rich element to the nutty flavor of the soba noodles.

Horenso Gomaae (Spinach with Sesame Dressing)

Ingredients:

- 1 bunch spinach
- 2 tablespoons white sesame seeds
- 1 tablespoon soy sauce
- 1 tablespoon sugar
- 1 tablespoon mirin
- 1 tablespoon sake
- Sesame oil (optional, for drizzling)

Instructions:

1. Prepare Spinach:

    Wash Spinach:
    - Wash the spinach thoroughly.

    Boil Water:
    - Bring a large pot of water to a boil.

    Blanch Spinach:
    - Add the spinach to the boiling water and blanch for about 1-2 minutes or until just wilted.

    Shock in Cold Water:
    - Quickly transfer the blanched spinach to a bowl of ice-cold water to stop the cooking process. Drain the spinach and squeeze out excess water.

2. Make Sesame Dressing:

    Toast Sesame Seeds:
    - In a dry pan over medium heat, toast the white sesame seeds until they become golden brown and aromatic. Be careful not to burn them.

    Grind Sesame Seeds:
    - Grind the toasted sesame seeds using a mortar and pestle or a food processor until you get a coarse paste.

    Make Dressing:

- In a bowl, combine the ground sesame seeds, soy sauce, sugar, mirin, and sake. Mix well to form a smooth dressing.

3. Dress Spinach:

    Coat Spinach:
    - Place the blanched and drained spinach in a bowl. Pour the sesame dressing over the spinach.

    Toss Gently:
    - Gently toss the spinach with the dressing until each leaf is coated.

4. Serve Horenso Gomaae:

    Plate Spinach:
    - Transfer the dressed spinach to a serving plate.

    Drizzle Sesame Oil (Optional):
    - Optionally, drizzle a small amount of sesame oil over the top for extra flavor.

    Serve at Room Temperature:
    - Horenso Gomaae can be served at room temperature, and it's a delightful side dish.

Note:

Horenso Gomaae is a classic Japanese side dish featuring blanched spinach dressed in a flavorful sesame dressing. The dressing is made from ground sesame seeds, soy sauce, sugar, mirin, and sake. The result is a nutty and savory flavor that perfectly complements the fresh taste of the spinach. This dish is not only delicious but also rich in nutrients. It's a popular addition to a traditional Japanese meal and can be served at room temperature or chilled.

Shrimp Shumai (steamed Shrimp Dumplings)

Ingredients:

For the Shrimp Filling:

- 1/2 pound (about 225g) shrimp, peeled and deveined
- 2 tablespoons bamboo shoots, finely chopped
- 2 tablespoons water chestnuts, finely chopped
- 1 green onion, finely chopped
- 1 tablespoon soy sauce
- 1 tablespoon oyster sauce
- 1 tablespoon sesame oil
- 1 teaspoon sugar
- 1/2 teaspoon ginger, grated
- 1/2 teaspoon garlic, minced
- Pinch of white pepper

For the Dumpling Wrapper:

- Round dumpling wrappers (store-bought or homemade)

For Garnish (Optional):

- Green onions, chopped
- Sesame seeds

Instructions:

1. Prepare Shrimp Filling:

    Chop Shrimp:
    - Finely chop the peeled and deveined shrimp into small pieces.

    Combine Ingredients:
    - In a bowl, mix the chopped shrimp with bamboo shoots, water chestnuts, green onion, soy sauce, oyster sauce, sesame oil, sugar, grated ginger, minced garlic, and white pepper. Mix well to combine.

2. Assemble Shrimp Shumai:

   Prepare Dumpling Wrappers:
   - If using store-bought dumpling wrappers, ensure they are thawed if frozen. If making homemade wrappers, roll the dough into small circles.

   Fill Wrappers:
   - Place a spoonful of the shrimp filling in the center of each dumpling wrapper.

   Shape Shumai:
   - Gather the edges of the wrapper around the filling, leaving the top open. Lightly press the edges to seal, creating a pleated pattern around the top. The shrimp filling should be exposed at the center.

3. Steam Shrimp Shumai:

   Prepare Steamer:
   - Arrange the shrimp shumai on a steamer lined with parchment paper or cabbage leaves.

   Steam:
   - Steam the shrimp shumai for about 8-10 minutes, or until the shrimp is cooked through and the wrappers are translucent.

4. Garnish and Serve:

   Garnish (Optional):
   - Garnish the steamed shrimp shumai with chopped green onions and sesame seeds if desired.

   Serve Warm:
   - Serve the shrimp shumai warm as an appetizer or part of a dim sum spread. They are delicious on their own or with a dipping sauce like soy sauce mixed with a bit of rice vinegar and chili oil.

Note:

Shrimp Shumai is a delightful and popular Chinese dim sum dish. These steamed shrimp dumplings feature a flavorful filling of chopped shrimp, bamboo shoots, water chestnuts, and seasonings. The dumplings are then wrapped in round wrappers and steamed to perfection. Shrimp shumai can be served as a tasty appetizer or as part of a dim sum feast. Enjoy their succulent and juicy texture along with the aromatic flavors of ginger, garlic, and sesame oil.

Kakiage (Vegetable Tempura Fritters)

Ingredients:

For the Tempura Batter:

- 1 cup all-purpose flour
- 1 tablespoon cornstarch
- 1 cup ice-cold water
- 1 egg
- Ice cubes

For the Vegetable Filling:

- 1 cup thinly sliced carrots
- 1 cup thinly sliced onions
- 1 cup thinly sliced bell peppers (assorted colors)
- 1 cup thinly sliced sweet potatoes
- 1 cup thinly sliced zucchini
- Other vegetables of your choice (e.g., mushrooms, green beans)

Vegetable options can be customized based on personal preference.

For Frying:

- Vegetable oil for deep-frying

For Dipping Sauce (Tentsuyu):

- 1/2 cup soy sauce
- 1/4 cup mirin
- 1/4 cup dashi (Japanese soup stock) or water
- 1 tablespoon sugar

Instructions:

1. Prepare Vegetables:

    Slice Vegetables:
    - Slice the vegetables into thin, uniform strips. Pat them dry with a paper towel to remove excess moisture.

2. Make Tempura Batter:

    Prepare Ice Water:
    - Fill a bowl with ice-cold water and add ice cubes.

    Make Batter:
    - In a mixing bowl, combine all-purpose flour and cornstarch. Gradually add ice-cold water while stirring. Beat in the egg and mix until you get a smooth batter. The batter should be thin.

3. Assemble Kakiage:

    Heat Oil:
    - Heat vegetable oil in a deep fryer or a large, deep pot to 350-375°F (180-190°C).

    Coat Vegetables:
    - Dip the sliced vegetables into the tempura batter, ensuring they are well coated.

    Form Fritters:
    - Gather a handful of coated vegetables and drop them into the hot oil, forming a loose ball. Repeat until you have a batch of kakiage.

    Fry Until Golden:
    - Fry the kakiage until golden brown and crispy. Make sure not to overcrowd the fryer or pot to maintain an even temperature.

    Drain Excess Oil:
    - Use a slotted spoon to remove the fried kakiage and place them on a plate lined with paper towels to drain excess oil.

    Repeat:
    - Repeat the process until all the vegetables are used.

4. Make Dipping Sauce (Tentsuyu):

Combine Ingredients:
- In a small saucepan, combine soy sauce, mirin, dashi (or water), and sugar. Heat over low heat until warmed through. Do not bring it to a boil.

5. Serve Kakiage:

Plate Kakiage:
- Arrange the kakiage on a serving plate.

Serve with Dipping Sauce:
- Serve the kakiage with the dipping sauce (tentsuyu) on the side.

Enjoy:
- Enjoy the crispy and delicious vegetable tempura fritters with the savory dipping sauce.

Note:

Kakiage is a delightful Japanese dish that features a mixture of thinly sliced vegetables coated in a light tempura batter and deep-fried until crispy. The assortment of vegetables adds a variety of flavors and textures to each bite. Serve kakiage with a tasty dipping sauce made from soy sauce, mirin, and dashi. It's a popular dish in Japan and makes for a delicious appetizer or snack.

Hijiki Salad (Seaweed Salad)

Ingredients:

- 1/2 cup dried hijiki seaweed
- 1 cup water (for soaking hijiki)
- 1 tablespoon vegetable oil
- 1 carrot, julienned
- 1/4 cup soy sauce
- 2 tablespoons mirin
- 1 tablespoon sugar
- 1 tablespoon rice vinegar
- 1 tablespoon sesame oil
- 1 tablespoon sesame seeds, toasted (for garnish)
- 2 green onions, finely chopped (for garnish)

Instructions:

1. Prepare Hijiki Seaweed:

    Soak Hijiki:
    - Place the dried hijiki seaweed in a bowl and cover it with 1 cup of water. Allow it to soak for about 15-20 minutes or until it becomes rehydrated.

    Drain and Squeeze:
    - Drain the rehydrated hijiki and gently squeeze out any excess water.

2. Cook Vegetables:

    Heat Vegetable Oil:
    - In a pan, heat vegetable oil over medium heat.

    Sauté Carrot:
    - Add the julienned carrot to the pan and sauté for 2-3 minutes until slightly softened.

3. Assemble Hijiki Salad:

    Combine Ingredients:

- Add the rehydrated hijiki to the pan with the sautéed carrots.

Make Sauce:
- In a small bowl, mix soy sauce, mirin, sugar, rice vinegar, and sesame oil to create the dressing.

Pour Dressing:
- Pour the dressing over the hijiki and carrot mixture. Stir well to combine.

4. Garnish and Serve:

Toast Sesame Seeds:
- In a dry pan, toast sesame seeds over medium heat until golden brown and fragrant.

Garnish with Sesame Seeds:
- Garnish the hijiki salad with toasted sesame seeds.

Add Green Onions:
- Sprinkle finely chopped green onions on top for added flavor and freshness.

Serve:
- Serve the hijiki salad at room temperature or chilled.

5. Enjoy:

- Enjoy this flavorful and nutritious seaweed salad as a side dish or a light appetizer.

Note:

Hijiki Salad is a traditional Japanese dish that features hijiki seaweed mixed with various ingredients to create a savory and slightly sweet salad. This dish is not only delicious but also rich in nutrients. The combination of rehydrated hijiki, sautéed carrots, and a flavorful dressing makes for a tasty and refreshing salad. Garnish with toasted sesame seeds and green onions for added texture and freshness. Serve it as a side dish or part of a Japanese meal.

Tori Momo (Chicken Thigh Skewers)

Ingredients:

- 1 pound boneless, skinless chicken thighs, cut into bite-sized pieces
- 1/4 cup soy sauce
- 2 tablespoons sake (Japanese rice wine)
- 2 tablespoons mirin
- 1 tablespoon sugar
- 1 tablespoon grated ginger
- 2 cloves garlic, minced
- Wooden skewers, soaked in water (to prevent burning)

Instructions:

1. Prepare Chicken:

    Cut Chicken Thighs:
    - Cut boneless, skinless chicken thighs into bite-sized pieces.

2. Make Marinade:

    Combine Ingredients:
    - In a bowl, mix soy sauce, sake, mirin, sugar, grated ginger, and minced garlic to create the marinade.

    Marinate Chicken:
    - Place the chicken pieces in the marinade and let them marinate for at least 30 minutes to allow the flavors to penetrate the meat.

3. Skewer Chicken:

    Preheat Grill or Broiler:
    - Preheat your grill or broiler.

    Skewer Chicken:
    - Thread the marinated chicken pieces onto the soaked wooden skewers.

4. Grill or Broil:

Cook Skewers:
- Grill or broil the chicken skewers for about 6-8 minutes, turning occasionally, until the chicken is cooked through and has a nice char.

5. Serve:

Garnish (Optional):
- Garnish with chopped green onions or sesame seeds if desired.

Serve Warm:
- Serve the Tori Momo hot as an appetizer or part of a meal.

3. Enjoy:

- Enjoy these flavorful and juicy chicken thigh skewers with your favorite dipping sauce or as is.

Note:

Tori Momo, or Chicken Thigh Skewers, is a popular yakitori (grilled chicken) dish in Japanese cuisine. The marinade, featuring soy sauce, sake, mirin, ginger, and garlic, imparts a savory and slightly sweet flavor to the chicken. Grilling or broiling the skewers gives the chicken a delicious char and a juicy texture. Tori Momo is a versatile dish that can be served as an appetizer, part of a meal, or even as a snack. Enjoy the rich umami taste of these skewers, either on their own or with your favorite dipping sauce.

Yaki Nasu (Grilled Eggplant)

Ingredients:

- 2 medium-sized Japanese or globe eggplants
- 2 tablespoons soy sauce
- 2 tablespoons mirin
- 1 tablespoon sake (Japanese rice wine)
- 1 tablespoon sugar
- Sesame seeds and chopped green onions for garnish (optional)

Instructions:

1. Prepare Eggplants:

    Cut Eggplants:
    - Cut the eggplants in half lengthwise.

2. Make Marinade:

    Combine Ingredients:
    - In a bowl, mix soy sauce, mirin, sake, and sugar to create the marinade.

3. Grill Eggplants:

    Preheat Grill or Broiler:
    - Preheat your grill or broiler.

    Brush with Marinade:
    - Brush the cut side of the eggplants with the marinade.

    Grill or Broil:
    - Grill or broil the eggplants with the cut side facing down for about 5-7 minutes, or until they are lightly charred and tender. Brush the skin side with the marinade.

    Flip and Cook:
    - Flip the eggplants and cook for an additional 5-7 minutes, brushing with more marinade as needed.

4. Serve:

    Garnish (Optional):

- Garnish the grilled eggplants with sesame seeds and chopped green onions if desired.

Serve Warm:
- Serve Yaki Nasu warm as a side dish or part of a Japanese meal.

3. Enjoy:

- Enjoy the smoky flavor and tender texture of the grilled eggplants with the savory-sweet marinade.

Note:

Yaki Nasu, or Grilled Eggplant, is a simple and delicious Japanese dish that highlights the natural flavor of eggplants with a savory-sweet marinade. The grilling process imparts a smoky aroma and tender texture to the eggplants. The marinade, made with soy sauce, mirin, sake, and sugar, adds depth and umami to the dish. Yaki Nasu can be served as a side dish, part of a bento box, or as an appetizer. Garnish with sesame seeds and green onions for added flavor and visual appeal.

Ise Ebi no Sashimi (Spiny Lobster Sashimi)

Ingredients:

- Fresh spiny lobster tails
- Soy sauce, for dipping
- Wasabi, for serving
- Pickled ginger, for serving

Instructions:

1. Select Fresh Spiny Lobster:

    Choose Quality Lobster:
    - Select fresh and high-quality spiny lobster tails for sashimi. Ensure that they are sourced from a reputable source.

2. Prepare Lobster Tails:

    Remove Meat:
    - Carefully remove the lobster meat from the shells. You can do this by cutting the tails open and extracting the meat.

    Slice for Sashimi:
    - Slice the lobster meat into thin sashimi-style pieces. It's important to use a sharp knife for clean cuts.

3. Serve:

    Arrange on Plate:
    - Arrange the spiny lobster sashimi slices on a serving plate.

    Serve with Condiments:
    - Serve the lobster sashimi with soy sauce on the side for dipping. Include wasabi and pickled ginger for additional flavor.

    Serve Chilled:
    - For the best experience, serve the spiny lobster sashimi chilled.

4. Enjoy:

    Savor the Delicacy:

- Enjoy the delicate and sweet flavor of spiny lobster sashimi. Dip each slice into soy sauce and add wasabi or pickled ginger according to your preference.

Note:

- Spiny lobster sashimi is a luxurious and delicately flavored dish. The fresh and tender lobster meat, served raw, allows you to experience the pure taste of this high-quality seafood. This dish is often enjoyed with minimal accompaniments to let the natural flavors shine. Always ensure that the lobster is sourced from a reliable and safe seafood provider to ensure freshness and quality.

Tako Sunomono (Octopus Vinegared Salad)

Ingredients:

- 1 cup cooked octopus, thinly sliced
- 1 cucumber, thinly sliced
- 1/4 cup rice vinegar
- 2 tablespoons soy sauce
- 1 tablespoon sugar
- 1 teaspoon mirin
- 1 teaspoon sesame oil
- Toasted sesame seeds for garnish
- Thinly sliced green onions for garnish

Instructions:

1. Prepare Octopus:

    Cook Octopus:
    - If using fresh octopus, clean and cook it according to your preferred method. Once cooked, thinly slice the octopus.

2. Make Vinegar Dressing:

    Combine Ingredients:
    - In a bowl, mix rice vinegar, soy sauce, sugar, mirin, and sesame oil to create the vinegar dressing.

    Stir Until Dissolved:
    - Stir the dressing until the sugar is completely dissolved.

3. Assemble Tako Sunomono:

    Combine Ingredients:
    - In a large bowl, combine the sliced octopus and cucumber.

    Pour Dressing:
    - Pour the vinegar dressing over the octopus and cucumber. Toss gently to ensure even coating.

4. Chill and Garnish:

>   Refrigerate:
>   - Cover the bowl and refrigerate the Tako Sunomono for at least 30 minutes to allow the flavors to meld.
>
>   Garnish:
>   - Before serving, garnish the salad with toasted sesame seeds and thinly sliced green onions.

5. Serve:

>   Plate and Enjoy:
>   - Serve Tako Sunomono chilled as a refreshing appetizer or side dish.
>
>   Enjoy the Delicate Flavor:
>   - Enjoy the delicate combination of tender octopus and crisp cucumber, enhanced by the savory-sweet vinegar dressing.

Note:

Tako Sunomono is a traditional Japanese dish that showcases thinly sliced octopus and cucumber in a refreshing vinegar-based dressing. The dish is both flavorful and light, making it a popular choice during warmer seasons. The combination of rice vinegar, soy sauce, sugar, mirin, and sesame oil creates a balanced and slightly sweet dressing that complements the seafood and vegetables. Garnishing with toasted sesame seeds and green onions adds extra depth and texture to the dish. Serve Tako Sunomono as an appetizer or a side dish for a delightful Japanese dining experience.

Inari Sushi (Sweet Soy-Marinated Tofu Pockets)

Ingredients:

- 1 cup sushi rice, cooked and seasoned with rice vinegar, sugar, and salt
- 8-10 inari age (seasoned tofu pockets)
- Soy sauce, for brushing
- Sesame seeds and sliced green onions for garnish (optional)

Instructions:

1. Prepare Sushi Rice:

    Cook Rice:
    - Cook sushi rice according to package instructions.

    Season Rice:
    - Season the cooked rice with a mixture of rice vinegar, sugar, and salt. Mix gently and let it cool to room temperature.

2. Prepare Inari Age:

    Open Tofu Pockets:
    - Carefully open the inari age (seasoned tofu pockets) without tearing them. They often come pre-cooked and seasoned in a sweet soy-based broth.

    Stuff with Sushi Rice:
    - Fill each tofu pocket with a small amount of sushi rice, pressing gently to pack it in.

    Brush with Soy Sauce:
    - Lightly brush the exterior of each inari sushi with soy sauce for added flavor.

3. Garnish and Serve:

    Garnish (Optional):
    - Garnish the top of each inari sushi with sesame seeds and sliced green onions for added texture and presentation.

    Serve:

- Arrange the Inari Sushi on a serving plate.

4. Enjoy:

    Serve and Enjoy:
    - Inari Sushi is now ready to be served. Enjoy these sweet and savory tofu pockets filled with delicious sushi rice.

Note:

Inari Sushi is a type of sushi that features seasoned tofu pockets filled with sushi rice. The tofu pockets, known as inari age, are typically sweet and savory due to being marinated in a soy-based broth. The sushi rice inside complements the flavors, creating a delightful bite-sized treat. Inari Sushi is often enjoyed as a light and convenient option for sushi lovers. Garnish with sesame seeds and green onions for added visual appeal.

Sake Harasu (Salmon Belly Sashimi)

Ingredients:

- Fresh salmon belly slices

For Dipping Sauce:

- Soy sauce
- Wasabi (optional)
- Pickled ginger (optional)

Instructions:

1. Select Fresh Salmon Belly:

    Choose Quality Salmon Belly:
    - Select fresh and high-quality salmon belly slices for sashimi. Ensure that they are sourced from a reputable fishmonger.

2. Prepare Salmon Belly:

    Slice Salmon Belly:
    - Using a sharp knife, thinly slice the salmon belly into sashimi-sized pieces.

3. Serve:

    Arrange on Plate:
    - Arrange the salmon belly slices on a serving plate.

    Serve with Dipping Sauce:
    - Serve the salmon belly sashimi with soy sauce on the side for dipping. Include wasabi and pickled ginger for additional flavor if desired.

4. Enjoy:

    Savor the Delicacy:
    - Enjoy the rich and buttery flavor of salmon belly sashimi. Dip each slice into soy sauce and add wasabi or pickled ginger according to your preference.

Note:

Sake Harasu, or Salmon Belly Sashimi, is a luxurious and indulgent dish that highlights the rich and buttery texture of the salmon belly. This sashimi is typically served raw to preserve its delicate flavor. Enjoy the slices on their own or with a simple dipping sauce made of soy sauce. Add wasabi and pickled ginger for a touch of heat and acidity. When preparing and consuming raw fish, it's crucial to source it from a reputable supplier to ensure freshness and quality.

Nikujaga Spring Rolls (Meat and Potato Spring Rolls)

Ingredients:

For Nikujaga Filling:

- 1 cup thinly sliced beef (such as thinly sliced ribeye or sirloin)
- 1 large potato, julienned
- 1 onion, thinly sliced
- 1 carrot, julienned
- 1 cup shirataki noodles, drained and cut into smaller pieces (optional)
- 2 tablespoons vegetable oil
- 2 tablespoons soy sauce
- 2 tablespoons mirin
- 1 tablespoon sake
- 1 tablespoon sugar
- 1 cup dashi (Japanese soup stock) or beef broth
- Salt and pepper to taste

For Spring Rolls:

- Spring roll wrappers
- Water (for sealing the wrappers)
- Vegetable oil (for frying)

Instructions:

1. Prepare Nikujaga Filling:

    Cook Beef:
    - In a pan, heat vegetable oil and sauté thinly sliced beef until browned.

    Add Vegetables:
    - Add julienned potato, sliced onion, julienned carrot, and shirataki noodles (if using). Cook until the vegetables are slightly softened.

    Season:
    - Add soy sauce, mirin, sake, sugar, and dashi (or beef broth) to the pan. Season with salt and pepper to taste. Simmer until the liquid reduces and the mixture is well-cooked.

    Cool Filling:
    - Allow the Nikujaga filling to cool completely before using it for spring rolls.

2. Assemble Nikujaga Spring Rolls:

    Prepare Spring Roll Wrappers:
    - Lay a spring roll wrapper on a clean surface with one corner pointing towards you. Keep a small bowl of water nearby for sealing.

    Add Filling:
    - Place a portion of the cooled Nikujaga filling on the bottom third of the wrapper.

    Roll Spring Rolls:
    - Fold the bottom corner over the filling, then fold in the sides, and roll up tightly.

    Seal Edges:
    - Use water to seal the edges of the spring roll.

3. Fry Spring Rolls:

    Heat Oil:
    - Heat vegetable oil in a pan or deep fryer to 350-375°F (180-190°C).

    Fry Until Golden:
    - Carefully place the Nikujaga spring rolls into the hot oil and fry until golden brown and crispy.

    Drain Excess Oil:
    - Use a slotted spoon to remove the fried spring rolls and place them on a paper towel-lined plate to drain excess oil.

4. Serve and Enjoy:

    Cut and Serve:
    - Allow the Nikujaga spring rolls to cool for a minute, then cut them into bite-sized pieces.

    Serve Warm:
    - Serve the Nikujaga spring rolls warm, perhaps with a dipping sauce of your choice.

Note:

Nikujaga Spring Rolls offer a unique twist by combining the flavors of the traditional Japanese dish Nikujaga (meat and potato stew) with the crispy and portable nature of spring rolls. The savory and slightly sweet Nikujaga filling, featuring beef, potatoes, and vegetables, is wrapped in spring roll wrappers and deep-fried to perfection. These rolls make for a delightful appetizer or snack, blending the comforting taste of Nikujaga with the satisfying crunch of spring rolls. Enjoy them with your favorite dipping sauce for an extra layer of flavor.

Miso Nasu (Miso-Glazed Eggplant)

Ingredients:

- 2 large Japanese eggplants
- 2 tablespoons white miso paste
- 2 tablespoons mirin
- 1 tablespoon soy sauce
- 1 tablespoon sugar
- 1 tablespoon sake
- 1 tablespoon vegetable oil
- Sesame seeds and green onions for garnish (optional)

Instructions:

1. Prepare Eggplants:

    Cut Eggplants:
    - Cut the eggplants in half lengthwise.

    Score and Salt:
    - Score the cut side of each eggplant half with a crisscross pattern. Sprinkle a little salt over the cut sides and let them sit for about 15 minutes. This helps remove excess moisture and bitterness.

2. Make Miso Glaze:

    Prepare Glaze:
    - In a bowl, whisk together white miso paste, mirin, soy sauce, sugar, and sake to create the miso glaze.

3. Grill or Broil Eggplants:

    Preheat Grill or Broiler:
    - Preheat your grill or broiler.

    Pat Dry and Brush with Oil:
    - Pat the eggplants dry with a paper towel. Brush the cut sides with vegetable oil.

Grill or Broil:
- Grill or broil the eggplants, cut side down, until the skin is charred, and the flesh is tender. This usually takes about 5-7 minutes.

4. Apply Miso Glaze:

Apply Miso Glaze:
- Flip the eggplants and brush the miso glaze over the cut sides. Continue grilling or broiling for an additional 2-3 minutes, allowing the glaze to caramelize.

5. Serve:

Garnish (Optional):
- Garnish the Miso Nasu with sesame seeds and chopped green onions if desired.

Serve Warm:
- Serve the Miso-Glazed Eggplant warm as a side dish or appetizer.

3. Enjoy:

Savor the Flavors:
- Enjoy the rich umami flavors of Miso Nasu, where the sweetness of miso glaze complements the smoky and tender eggplant.

Note:

Miso Nasu, or Miso-Glazed Eggplant, is a classic Japanese dish that showcases the natural sweetness of eggplant enhanced by a flavorful miso-based glaze. The eggplants are grilled or broiled until tender, and then brushed with a mixture of white miso paste, mirin, soy sauce, sugar, and sake. This creates a caramelized and savory coating that elevates the dish. Garnish with sesame seeds and green onions for added texture and freshness. Serve Miso Nasu as a side dish or appetizer, and enjoy the delightful combination of smoky, sweet, and savory flavors.

Kushiage (Deep-Fried Skewers)

Ingredients:

For Kushiage:

- Assorted ingredients for skewering (e.g., meat, vegetables, seafood)
- Wooden skewers, soaked in water
- Flour, for coating
- Eggs, beaten
- Panko breadcrumbs
- Vegetable oil, for deep-frying

For Dipping Sauce:

- 1/4 cup soy sauce
- 2 tablespoons mirin
- 1 tablespoon sake
- 1 tablespoon sugar

Instructions:

1. Prepare Ingredients:

    Cut Ingredients:
    - Cut your choice of ingredients into bite-sized pieces suitable for skewering, such as meat, vegetables, and seafood.

    Skewer Ingredients:
    - Thread the prepared ingredients onto the soaked wooden skewers.

2. Set Up Breading Station:

    Prepare Coating Ingredients:
    - Place flour, beaten eggs, and panko breadcrumbs in separate shallow dishes.

3. Coat and Bread Skewers:

    Coat with Flour:

- Roll each skewer in flour, shaking off excess.

Dip in Beaten Eggs:
- Dip the floured skewers into the beaten eggs, ensuring an even coating.

Cover with Panko:
- Roll the skewers in panko breadcrumbs, pressing gently to adhere the breadcrumbs.

4. Fry Kushiage:

Heat Oil:
- In a deep fryer or large, deep pan, heat vegetable oil to 350-375°F (180-190°C).

Deep-Fry Skewers:
- Carefully place the skewers into the hot oil and fry until golden brown and crispy. Fry in batches to avoid overcrowding.

Drain Excess Oil:
- Use a slotted spoon to remove the fried skewers and place them on a paper towel-lined plate to drain excess oil.

5. Prepare Dipping Sauce:

Combine Sauce Ingredients:
- In a small bowl, mix soy sauce, mirin, sake, and sugar to create the dipping sauce. Stir until the sugar dissolves.

6. Serve:

Arrange and Serve:
- Arrange the Kushiage on a serving platter and serve with the dipping sauce on the side.

Enjoy:
- Enjoy the crispy and flavorful Kushiage with the dipping sauce. Serve as an appetizer or part of a meal.

Note:

Kushiage, or deep-fried skewers, is a popular Japanese dish that allows for a variety of ingredients to be skewered, coated, and deep-fried until golden and crispy. The assortment of ingredients can include meat, vegetables, and seafood. The breading process involves coating the skewers with flour, dipping them in beaten eggs, and covering them in panko breadcrumbs for a crunchy texture. Serve Kushiage with a savory dipping sauce to complement the fried goodness. It's a delightful and customizable dish perfect for sharing or as a unique appetizer.

Wakame Salad (Seaweed Salad)

Ingredients:

- 1 cup dried wakame seaweed
- 2 tablespoons soy sauce
- 1 tablespoon sesame oil
- 1 tablespoon rice vinegar
- 1 tablespoon mirin
- 1 teaspoon sugar
- 1 teaspoon grated ginger
- 1 teaspoon sesame seeds (optional)
- Thinly sliced cucumber (optional, for added freshness)
- Sliced radishes (optional, for garnish)

Instructions:

1. Rehydrate Wakame:

    Soak Wakame:
    - Place the dried wakame seaweed in a bowl and soak it in warm water for about 10-15 minutes or until it rehydrates and becomes tender.

    Drain and Squeeze:
    - Drain the rehydrated wakame and gently squeeze out excess water.

2. Prepare Dressing:

    Whisk Ingredients:
    - In a bowl, whisk together soy sauce, sesame oil, rice vinegar, mirin, sugar, and grated ginger to create the dressing.

3. Combine Salad Ingredients:

    Mix Wakame and Dressing:
    - In a large bowl, combine the rehydrated wakame with the prepared dressing. Toss gently to coat the seaweed evenly.

    Optional Additions:
    - Add thinly sliced cucumber for freshness and additional crunch. Toss to combine.

4. Garnish and Serve:

    Chill:
    - Refrigerate the Wakame Salad for at least 30 minutes to allow the flavors to meld.

    Garnish:
    - Before serving, garnish the salad with optional sliced radishes and sprinkle with sesame seeds if desired.

5. Serve and Enjoy:

    Serve Cold:
    - Serve Wakame Salad cold as a refreshing side dish or appetizer.

    Enjoy the Umami Flavor:
    - Enjoy the umami-rich flavor of the seaweed combined with the savory-sweet dressing.

Note:

Wakame Salad, also known as Seaweed Salad, is a light and refreshing Japanese dish that features rehydrated wakame seaweed tossed in a flavorful dressing. The dressing combines soy sauce, sesame oil, rice vinegar, mirin, sugar, and grated ginger to create a harmonious balance of savory, sweet, and umami flavors. Optionally, add thinly sliced cucumber for freshness and radishes for a colorful garnish. Serve this chilled salad as a delightful side dish or appetizer, perfect for enjoying the unique taste of seaweed.

Uni Gunkan (Sea Urchin Battleship Sushi)

Ingredients:

- Sushi rice (prepared with rice vinegar, sugar, and salt)
- Fresh sea urchin (uni)
- Nori (seaweed) strips
- Soy sauce (for dipping)
- Wasabi (optional, for serving)

Instructions:

1. Prepare Sushi Rice:

    Cook Rice:
    - Cook sushi rice according to package instructions.

    Season Rice:
    - While the rice is still warm, gently fold in a mixture of rice vinegar, sugar, and salt to season it. Allow the rice to cool to room temperature.

2. Assemble Uni Gunkan:

    Prepare Nori Strips:
    - Cut nori sheets into thin strips to wrap around the sushi rice.

    Form Rice:
    - Take a small amount of sushi rice and form it into an oval shape, creating a small bed for the sea urchin.

    Wrap with Nori:
    - Wrap a strip of nori around the sides of the rice to create a "battleship" shape, leaving the top open.

    Add Sea Urchin (Uni):
    - Place a generous amount of fresh sea urchin (uni) on top of the rice bed.

3. Serve Uni Gunkan:

    Arrange on Plate:
    - Arrange the Uni Gunkan on a serving plate.

Serve with Soy Sauce and Wasabi:
- Serve the Uni Gunkan with soy sauce for dipping and wasabi on the side if desired.

3. Enjoy:

Savor the Delicacy:
- Enjoy the unique and delicate flavor of sea urchin in this delightful sushi creation.

Note:

Uni Gunkan, also known as Sea Urchin Battleship Sushi, is a sushi style that features fresh sea urchin served on a small bed of seasoned sushi rice and wrapped with a strip of nori to create a "battleship" shape. The nori acts as a vessel to hold the sea urchin in place, allowing you to enjoy its rich and delicate flavor. Serve Uni Gunkan with soy sauce for dipping and optional wasabi on the side. This sushi variation is a true delicacy, appreciated for its unique taste and elegant presentation.

Yaki Onigiri (Grilled Rice Balls)

Ingredients:

- Cooked sushi rice (short-grain rice)
- Soy sauce
- Nori sheets, cut into thin strips (optional)
- Salt (for sprinkling)
- Vegetable oil (for brushing)

Instructions:

1. Prepare Sushi Rice:

    Cook Rice:
    - Cook short-grain sushi rice according to package instructions.

    Shape Rice Balls:
    - Once the rice is cooked, let it cool slightly. Wet your hands to prevent sticking and shape the rice into small, compact triangles or balls.

2. Grill Rice Balls:

    Preheat Grill or Pan:
    - Preheat a grill or a non-stick pan over medium heat.

    Brush with Oil:
    - Brush the shaped rice balls with a thin layer of vegetable oil to prevent sticking and promote a crispy exterior.

    Grill Until Golden:
    - Place the rice balls on the grill or in the pan. Grill each side until golden brown and crispy. This usually takes about 2-3 minutes per side.

    Brush with Soy Sauce:
    - During the last minute of grilling, brush the rice balls with soy sauce for added flavor. Rotate and continue grilling until the desired crispiness is achieved.

3. Serve Yaki Onigiri:

Optional Nori Garnish:
- If desired, wrap thin strips of nori around the grilled rice balls for additional flavor and presentation.

Sprinkle with Salt:
- Sprinkle a pinch of salt over the grilled onigiri for extra seasoning.

4. Enjoy:

Serve Warm:
- Serve Yaki Onigiri warm as a delicious and crispy snack or as a side dish.

Savor the Crispy Texture:
- Enjoy the contrast of the crispy exterior and tender interior of the grilled rice balls.

Note:

Yaki Onigiri, or Grilled Rice Balls, is a simple and flavorful dish that involves grilling shaped rice balls until they develop a crispy exterior. The use of short-grain sushi rice is ideal for achieving the desired texture. Brushing the rice balls with oil before grilling helps create a golden and crispy crust. During the grilling process, brushing with soy sauce adds a savory flavor to the onigiri. Garnishing with nori strips and a sprinkle of salt enhances the overall taste. Serve Yaki Onigiri warm as a delightful snack or as a side dish to complement various meals.

Kinoko Butter Yaki (Butter-Sautéed Mushrooms)

Ingredients:

- Assorted mushrooms (shiitake, maitake, enoki, shimeji, or your choice)
- Butter
- Soy sauce
- Mirin
- Sake
- Green onions, finely chopped (for garnish)
- Sesame seeds (optional, for garnish)

Instructions:

1. Prepare Mushrooms:

    Clean and Trim Mushrooms:
    - Clean the mushrooms and trim any tough stems. If using larger mushrooms like shiitake, slice them into bite-sized pieces.

2. Cook Mushrooms:

    Melt Butter:
    - In a pan, melt a generous amount of butter over medium heat.

    Sauté Mushrooms:
    - Add the prepared mushrooms to the pan and sauté until they start to brown and become tender.

3. Make Sauce:

    Add Soy Sauce, Mirin, and Sake:
    - Pour in a splash of soy sauce, mirin, and sake. Adjust the quantities based on your taste preferences.

    Simmer:
    - Allow the mushrooms to simmer in the sauce, absorbing the flavors, and cook until the liquid is reduced.

4. Garnish and Serve:

> Garnish:
> - Sprinkle finely chopped green onions and sesame seeds (if using) over the mushrooms for garnish.
>
> Serve Warm:
> - Serve Kinoko Butter Yaki warm as a side dish or topping for rice.

3. Enjoy:

> Savor the Flavor:
> - Enjoy the rich and savory flavor of butter-sautéed mushrooms with the added depth from soy sauce, mirin, and sake.

Note:

Kinoko Butter Yaki is a delicious Japanese dish that highlights the natural umami of assorted mushrooms sautéed in butter. The combination of soy sauce, mirin, and sake enhances the savory flavor profile. You can use a mix of mushrooms such as shiitake, maitake, enoki, shimeji, or your preferred varieties. The dish is finished with a garnish of finely chopped green onions and optional sesame seeds. Serve Kinoko Butter Yaki as a delightful side dish or on top of rice for a comforting and flavorful experience.

Takoyaki (Octopus Balls)

Ingredients:

For Takoyaki Batter:

- 2 cups takoyaki flour (or all-purpose flour)
- 4 large eggs
- 4 cups dashi (Japanese soup stock)
- 1/2 teaspoon salt

For Filling:

- Cooked octopus pieces (small bite-sized)
- Tenkasu (tempura scraps)
- Green onions, finely chopped
- Pickled red ginger (beni shoga)

For Takoyaki Sauce:

- 1/3 cup Worcestershire sauce
- 2 tablespoons soy sauce
- 1 tablespoon mirin
- 1 tablespoon sugar

For Toppings:

- Bonito flakes (katsuobushi)
- Aonori (seaweed flakes)

For Garnish:

- Japanese mayonnaise

Instructions:

1. Prepare Takoyaki Batter:

    Combine Ingredients:
    - In a large bowl, whisk together takoyaki flour, eggs, dashi, and salt until the batter is smooth.

2. Cook Takoyaki:

    Preheat Takoyaki Pan:
    - Preheat a takoyaki pan over medium heat.

    Grease the Pan:
    - Grease the takoyaki pan with a small amount of oil.

    Pour Batter:
    - Pour the batter into the takoyaki pan, filling each mold almost to the top.

    Add Filling:
    - Place a small piece of cooked octopus, tenkasu, chopped green onions, and a bit of pickled red ginger in each mold.

    Cook and Flip:
    - As the edges start to cook, use a skewer or takoyaki pick to flip each takoyaki ball, forming a round shape. Continue cooking and turning until they are golden brown and cooked through.

3. Make Takoyaki Sauce:

    Combine Sauce Ingredients:
    - In a small saucepan, combine Worcestershire sauce, soy sauce, mirin, and sugar. Heat over low heat until well combined and heated through.

4. Serve Takoyaki:

    Drizzle with Sauce:
    - Drizzle the takoyaki sauce over the cooked takoyaki.

    Top with Bonito Flakes and Aonori:
    - Sprinkle bonito flakes and aonori over the top.

    Add Japanese Mayonnaise:
    - Finish by drizzling Japanese mayonnaise over the takoyaki.

5. Enjoy:

   Serve Hot:
   - Serve the Takoyaki hot, and enjoy the crispy exterior with the tender octopus filling.

Note:

Takoyaki, or Octopus Balls, is a popular Japanese street food known for its crispy exterior and gooey interior. The batter is made with takoyaki flour, eggs, dashi, and salt. The filling typically includes cooked octopus pieces, tenkasu (tempura scraps), green onions, and pickled red ginger. The takoyaki are cooked in a special takoyaki pan, and once golden brown, they are drizzled with a savory takoyaki sauce, topped with bonito flakes and aonori (seaweed flakes), and finished with Japanese mayonnaise. Serve Takoyaki hot for a delicious and satisfying treat.

Yudofu (Hot Tofu)

Ingredients:

- 14 ounces (400g) firm tofu
- 4 cups dashi (Japanese soup stock)
- 1/4 cup soy sauce
- 2 tablespoons mirin
- 2 green onions, finely chopped (for garnish)
- Grated ginger (for garnish, optional)
- Shichimi togarashi (Japanese seven spice, optional)

Instructions:

1. Prepare Tofu:

    Drain Tofu:
    - Remove the tofu from the packaging, drain excess water, and cut it into bite-sized cubes.

2. Prepare Dashi Broth:

    Heat Dashi:
    - In a pot, heat the dashi over medium heat. Bring it to a simmer, but avoid boiling.

    Add Soy Sauce and Mirin:
    - Stir in soy sauce and mirin into the dashi, mixing well.

3. Cook Tofu in Dashi:

    Add Tofu:
    - Gently place the tofu cubes into the simmering dashi.

    Simmer:
    - Let the tofu simmer in the broth for about 5-7 minutes, allowing it to absorb the flavors.

4. Serve Yudofu:

Ladle into Bowls:
- Use a ladle to transfer the hot tofu and dashi broth into serving bowls.

Garnish:
- Garnish with finely chopped green onions and grated ginger if desired.

Optional Spice:
- Sprinkle a bit of shichimi togarashi (Japanese seven spice) over the top for added spice, if you like.

5. Enjoy:

Serve Hot:
- Serve Yudofu hot as a comforting and simple Japanese tofu dish.

Note:

Yudofu, or Hot Tofu, is a traditional Japanese dish that highlights the delicate flavors of tofu. In this dish, firm tofu is gently simmered in a savory broth made with dashi, soy sauce, and mirin. The result is a simple and comforting hot tofu dish that allows the purity of the tofu to shine. Garnish with green onions and grated ginger for freshness and optional shichimi togarashi for a hint of spice. Yudofu is often enjoyed as a light and soothing meal, especially during colder seasons.

Saba Misoni (Miso-Braised Mackerel)

Ingredients:

- 2 mackerel fillets, cleaned and cut into serving pieces
- 1/4 cup sake (Japanese rice wine)
- 1/4 cup mirin (sweet rice wine)
- 3 tablespoons sugar
- 3 tablespoons miso paste
- 1 tablespoon soy sauce
- 1 tablespoon vegetable oil
- 1 green onion, chopped (for garnish)

Instructions:

1. Prepare Mackerel:

    Clean Mackerel:
    - Clean the mackerel fillets and cut them into serving-sized pieces.

2. Make Miso-Braising Sauce:

    Mix Sauce Ingredients:
    - In a bowl, whisk together sake, mirin, sugar, miso paste, and soy sauce to create the miso-braising sauce.

3. Braise Mackerel:

    Heat Vegetable Oil:
    - In a large pan, heat vegetable oil over medium heat.

    Sear Mackerel:
    - Sear the mackerel fillets on both sides until lightly browned.

    Add Sauce:
    - Pour the miso-braising sauce over the mackerel fillets in the pan.

    Simmer:
    - Lower the heat and let the mackerel simmer in the sauce for about 10-15 minutes, or until the fish is cooked through and the sauce has thickened.

4. Garnish and Serve:

Garnish:
- Garnish with chopped green onions.

Serve Hot:
- Serve Saba Misoni hot over rice or as a main dish.

5. Enjoy:

Savor the Flavor:
- Enjoy the rich and savory flavor of the miso-braised mackerel.

Note:

Saba Misoni, or Miso-Braised Mackerel, is a classic Japanese dish where mackerel fillets are braised in a flavorful miso-based sauce. The sauce combines the sweetness of mirin, the depth of sake, the umami of miso paste, and the savory touch of soy sauce. The mackerel is seared and then simmered in the sauce until it absorbs the rich flavors. Garnish with chopped green onions for a fresh contrast. Saba Misoni is typically served hot over rice and is known for its comforting and satisfying taste.

Nasu Dengaku (Miso-Glazed Eggplant)

Ingredients:

- 2 medium-sized Japanese eggplants
- 2 tablespoons white miso paste
- 1 tablespoon mirin
- 1 tablespoon sake
- 1 tablespoon sugar
- 1 tablespoon vegetable oil
- Sesame seeds and chopped green onions (for garnish)

Instructions:

1. Prepare Eggplant:

    Cut Eggplants:
    - Cut the Japanese eggplants in half lengthwise.

    Score the Flesh:
    - Using a knife, score the flesh of the eggplants in a crisscross pattern, making sure not to cut through the skin.

2. Make Miso Glaze:

    Mix Glaze Ingredients:
    - In a bowl, whisk together white miso paste, mirin, sake, and sugar to create the miso glaze.

3. Glaze and Grill Eggplant:

    Brush with Oil:
    - Brush the cut side of the eggplants with vegetable oil.

    Grill or Broil:
    - Grill or broil the eggplants, cut side down, until they are slightly charred and tender.

    Apply Miso Glaze:
    - Flip the eggplants and generously brush the miso glaze on the scored side.

    Continue Cooking:

- Continue grilling or broiling until the miso glaze caramelizes and the eggplants are fully cooked.

4. Garnish and Serve:

   Garnish:
   - Sprinkle sesame seeds and chopped green onions over the glazed eggplants for garnish.

   Serve Hot:
   - Serve Nasu Dengaku hot as a delicious appetizer or side dish.

5. Enjoy:

   Savor the Flavor:
   - Enjoy the sweet and savory flavors of the miso-glazed eggplant.

Note:

Nasu Dengaku, or Miso-Glazed Eggplant, is a popular Japanese dish known for its sweet and savory flavor. Japanese eggplants are halved, scored, and grilled or broiled until tender and slightly charred. The miso glaze, made with white miso paste, mirin, sake, and sugar, is generously brushed onto the eggplants and caramelizes during cooking, creating a delicious coating. Garnish with sesame seeds and chopped green onions for added flavor and presentation. Nasu Dengaku is often served as an appetizer or side dish, showcasing the rich taste of miso with the smoky goodness of grilled eggplant.

Ginnan (Ginkgo Nuts)

Ingredients:

- Fresh ginkgo nuts in their shells

Instructions:

1. Shelling Ginkgo Nuts:

    Harvest or Purchase Fresh Ginkgo Nuts:
    - Harvest or purchase fresh ginkgo nuts while they are in season.

    Wear Gloves (Optional):
    - If you're sensitive to the resin on the shells, wear gloves to protect your hands.

    Remove Outer Shell:
    - Use a small knife to carefully cut through the outer shell of the ginkgo nut.

    Extract Inner Nut:
    - Extract the inner nut from the shell. The inner nut is edible, while the outer fleshy part is not.

2. Roasting Ginkgo Nuts:

    Preheat Oven:
    - Preheat your oven to 350°F (175°C).

    Spread Nuts on Baking Sheet:
    - Place the shelled ginkgo nuts on a baking sheet in a single layer.

    Roast in Oven:
    - Roast the ginkgo nuts in the preheated oven for about 15-20 minutes or until they become golden brown.

    Check for Doneness:
    - Check the nuts regularly, and shake the pan to ensure even roasting.

    Cool and Serve:
    - Once roasted, let the ginkgo nuts cool before serving.

3. Enjoy:

    Crack and Eat:
    - Crack open the roasted ginkgo nuts to reveal the inner edible part. Discard the outer shell.

Savor the Nutty Flavor:
- Enjoy the nutty flavor of freshly roasted ginkgo nuts.

Note:

Ginnan, or ginkgo nuts, can be enjoyed by roasting them for a delicious and nutty flavor. Harvest or purchase fresh ginkgo nuts, and carefully extract the inner nut from the outer shell. Roast the shelled ginkgo nuts in the oven until they turn golden brown. Once roasted, crack open the nuts and discard the outer shell, revealing the edible inner part. Ginkgo nuts are often enjoyed as a seasonal snack, and roasting enhances their natural nutty taste.

Tamagoyaki (Japanese Sweet Omelette)

Ingredients:

- 4 large eggs
- 2 tablespoons sugar
- 1 tablespoon soy sauce
- 1 tablespoon mirin
- 1/2 teaspoon salt
- Vegetable oil for greasing the pan

Instructions:

1. Prepare Tamagoyaki Mixture:

    Whisk Eggs:
    - In a bowl, whisk the eggs until well beaten.

    Add Sugar, Soy Sauce, Mirin, and Salt:
    - Add sugar, soy sauce, mirin, and salt to the beaten eggs. Whisk thoroughly to ensure the sugar is dissolved.

2. Cook Tamagoyaki:

    Heat Tamagoyaki Pan:
    - Heat a tamagoyaki pan (rectangular omelette pan) over medium heat. Brush the pan with a thin layer of vegetable oil.

    Pour a Thin Layer of Egg Mixture:
    - Pour a thin layer of the egg mixture into the pan, enough to cover the bottom.

    Roll the Omelette:
    - Once the bottom is set but still slightly runny on top, start rolling the omelette from one end to the other using chopsticks or a spatula.

    Move Rolled Omelette to the Opposite End:
    - Move the rolled omelette to the opposite end of the pan.

    Oil the Empty Part of the Pan:
    - Brush the empty part of the pan with oil, and pour another thin layer of the egg mixture to cover the bottom.

    Lift the Rolled Omelette and Let the New Mixture Flow Underneath:
    - Lift the rolled omelette slightly to let the new egg mixture flow underneath.

Roll Again:
- Once the new layer is set but still slightly runny, roll the omelette again towards the end of the pan.

Repeat Steps 4-7:
- Repeat the process of oiling the empty part, pouring egg mixture, and rolling until all the egg mixture is used.

3. Finish and Slice:

Finish Rolling:
- Once you've used all the egg mixture and have a rolled omelette, let it cook for a minute or two to ensure it's fully set.

Remove from Pan and Cool:
- Remove the tamagoyaki from the pan and let it cool on a bamboo mat or a cutting board with the seam side down.

Slice and Serve:
- Slice the tamagoyaki into bite-sized pieces and serve. Optionally, you can wrap it in a bamboo sushi rolling mat while it cools to help maintain its shape.

4. Enjoy:

Serve Warm or at Room Temperature:
- Tamagoyaki can be served warm or at room temperature. Enjoy the sweet and savory flavors of this Japanese sweet omelette.

Note:

Tamagoyaki, a Japanese sweet omelette, is a popular dish often served for breakfast or as a side dish. The sweet and savory flavor comes from the combination of sugar, soy sauce, and mirin. Cooking it in layers and rolling it creates a unique texture. It's commonly enjoyed on its own, in sushi, or as a topping for rice.

Hokkigai Sashimi (Surf Clam Sashimi)

Ingredients:

- Fresh hokkigai (surf clam) meat
- Soy sauce, for dipping
- Wasabi, for serving
- Pickled ginger (gari), for serving

Instructions:

1. Purchase Fresh Hokkigai:

    Select Quality Surf Clams:
    - Choose fresh and high-quality hokkigai (surf clam) from a reputable seafood source.

2. Prepare Surf Clam Meat:

    Clean and Slice:
    - Clean the hokkigai thoroughly and slice the meat into thin sashimi-style pieces.

3. Arrange on Serving Plate:

    Artistically Arrange:
    - Arrange the hokkigai slices on a serving plate, creating an appealing presentation.

4. Serve:

    Serve with Accompaniments:
    - Serve the hokkigai sashimi with soy sauce for dipping, wasabi for added spice, and pickled ginger (gari) to cleanse the palate between bites.

5. Enjoy:

Savor the Freshness:
- Enjoy the clean and briny flavor of hokkigai sashimi, appreciating its fresh and delicate taste.

Note:

Hokkigai Sashimi, featuring surf clam slices, is a delightful and refreshing dish commonly found in Japanese cuisine. To prepare, select high-quality and fresh hokkigai from a reliable seafood source. Clean and slice the surf clam meat into thin, elegant pieces. Arrange the slices on a serving plate in an appealing manner. Serve the hokkigai sashimi with soy sauce for dipping, wasabi for a touch of heat, and pickled ginger (gari) to cleanse the palate. Savor the clean and briny taste of hokkigai sashimi as a delightful addition to your sushi or sashimi experience.

www.ingramcontent.com/pod-product-compliance
Lightning Source LLC
LaVergne TN
LVHW081552060526
838201LV00054B/1878